Four Walls of Stone

by

Kimeko R. Campbell

Four Walls of Stone

Kimeko Campbell

Los Angeles, CA

Kimekorenee@aol.com

Ordering Information:

Special discounts are available on quantity purchases by corporations, associations, educational institutions, and others. For details, contact Kimeko Campbell above.

Printed in the United States of America

First Edition

ISBN# 978-1-5136-9611-9

Publisher: Winsome Entertainment Group LLC

Introduction

To those who are taking the time to read this book, I thank you for your support and I pray that you are blessed and never have to experience any time in jail or prison, ever. However, if you do make a mistake and end up there, don't ever give up hope. Look out of that tiny window in your cell (if you are lucky enough to have one in your cell) and keep hope alive through faith in God. Trust me, if or when you are imprisoned in any situation, God is your very best friend. Everybody calls on God when they are desperate, no matter their beliefs.

In fact, many people, especially good ole Americans, have spent time in jail or prison. I can't count the number of celebrities who have done time in the "Big House." Even if they got bailed out within hours, they still experienced the stench and degradation of being locked in a jail cell and restricted of their dignity and pride. Even the whole Simpson's cartoon family has been to jail.

Money does help and goes a long way when it comes to legal representation, I am proof of that. I had no money and received the worst legal defense in the history of mankind. If I would have had the money to hire a private attorney, the case would have certainly been dismissed. Had I been Caucasian, I would have never been arrested. There are most definitely two justice systems: one for rich people, one for poor people.

Rich people can afford to hire the best lawyers. The courts and the judicial system recognize private lawyers but not public defenders.

Courts do not respect anyone who is being represented by a public defender. Have you ever heard of a public defender winning a case?

This is my story about my stay in prison. Thank you for allowing me to share this part of my life with you. I hope it helps any and everyone who reads it have a better understanding of any situation that they may currently be facing. Or at least help you avoid facing a similar situation to mine. I call it my prison stay-cation, my journey to another world and what a different world it was. This was no doubt the most uncertain, tumultuous, scariest, exciting, surreal, humbling time in my entire life thus far. Even though I made it through fairly smoothly, I am so very grateful that this particular part of my life is over. "That too did pass."

Praise God Almighty.

Chapter 1

A Matter of a Squirrel

On a beautiful California evening, in the early spring of 2002, I was driving my Jeep Wrangler with my niece, on our way to get burgers. Out of the blue, I got a phone call from someone who owed me money for a squirrel that I had sold her – a six-month-old ground squirrel that I could no longer provide for.

Perfect timing. I was heading in her direction and could use the $25 that she had for me, for our burgers. I told my niece that it was her friend Tisha that I was talking to on the telephone, and she had money for me. My niece told me that she didn't think Tisha would ever pay me at all. Tisha told me that she and her boyfriend had moved into a new apartment, so she gave me her address and we went to her new apartment.

Little did I knew that things wouldn't turn out to be that simple. That beautiful evening turned out to be the worst night of my life. My entire life changed forever and would never be the same. From that point on, I would never trust anyone, especially anyone in my entire family, again.

We arrived and I rang the buzzer. I had a bad feeling and almost left. If only I had listened to my first thought which was to leave after they didn't answer the buzzer. But then, Tisha's boyfriend came down the stairs and opened the door and let me in. I could feel some tension but didn't follow my instinct to leave and that was a huge mistake.

As soon as I walked into their apartment, I felt gloom. It was dark and it felt weird. Then, Tisha's boyfriend started pacing back and forth and was saying things like, "I know this bitch didn't come over here for no money." He had his fist balled up and he was punching the palm of his hand.

I said, "The only bitch in here is you."

At that, he went off and punched me hard!

I think I was unconscious for a few seconds because I remember seeing stars. I came to and I had no idea what was really happening. He was on top of me, and I was either fighting back or trying to grab his arms to stop him from hitting me. He kept striking me in my head with something.

I barely managed to escape with my life. I ran to my Jeep and was so discombobulated that I didn't know what to do. I thought that he might come after me or I would pass out. I didn't know whether to go to the hospital or the police station.

There are so many things that I wish I had done differently that night. But I have to believe that everything happens for a reason. One of the reasons that I am writing this book is with hopes that it will touch its readers and help them avoid going to jail or prison. My major advice to my readers is to take the time to re-think a situation before it becomes dangerous. Follow your first instinct and think about the worst consequences that can develop from the incident. If that doesn't stop you, at least make sure that you can afford to hire a good lawyer and be sure to exercise all your rights, especially your right to remain silent. Once the police get a statement or confession from you that is it. You're dead meat to them. The next time you see them will be in court and they will be using every single thing that you told them to testify against you, with no mercy.

Chapter 2

Day of Reckoning

July 3, 2002.

The day that has been haunting me for the past three months. Today is the day that kept me up all night worrying. Today is a day full of uncertainty. Today is the day that my life completely changes. Today is the day that I lose everything for nothing. Today is the day that the verdict in my case will be read. Today is the day that I am found guilty of all charges against me. Today is the day that I am sentenced to eighteen months in prison.

Today was the first day of my sentence and just like in the movies, I marked the wall with a pencil. Today is Day One of a 547.501-day sentence. Can you imagine that? Today was not a good day, at all.

That douche bag, turd sandwich, judge screamed at me as he read out the verdict for my case. Calling me a monster when he totally had the baboon by the tail. Nothing about that crime was even closely related to me being a monster. I was the victim. One day you will be judged and sent to jail. Jackass. As I sat there in disbelief that I was actually going to jail, and that my life was over. All I could do was cry. I never thought things would get that far.

When you see people crying after they have been convicted, they are most likely innocent. They are crying because they have been wrongly convicted. Guilty people never cry. Most guilty people can't cry. Even when they try to cry, nothing comes out. Innocent people cry rivers. I have never seen one person who was being charged with killing his family or raping a child, shed one tear. For example, Scott Peterson or Chris Watts never shed a tear. Daniel Holtzclaw cried his heart out. Serial killers, child rapists, baby killers, etc., don't ever cry and the judge and jury still have sympathy for them. Shame on those judges and jurors. Let this be a note to you, that one day it could be you.

I had absolutely no criminal history whatsoever, and when I was arrested, all of my rights were violated. I had no intention of getting into any kind confrontation with anyone the night that I was arrested. Had I known I was going to have to fight for my life over $25, I would have taken my brother with me. My brother was 6'3' and would have ripped that punk to pieces, especially if I paid him $25 to do it.

I couldn't afford an attorney because once I was arrested and taken to jail, I asked my sister Tia, to go to my house and get money out of my safe and bail me out of jail. She did get the money and bail me out of jail, but a few days later, she and two of my nephews broke into my apartment while I was at church with my mother. They stole the rest of my money. They took my whole safe. The safe was later found by the police, in my oldest sister's back yard. It had their fingerprints all over it.

I had $14,000 stolen from me by three of my family members. I soon found out that just about all my family members were in on it. I was beyond devastated. It was worse than a nightmare. I was out of jail on bail and couldn't afford an attorney. And I couldn't trust anyone in my entire family. I was all on my own and I had absolutely nowhere to go. I needed a serious vacation from my life at that time. I wouldn't even call that a life. That was an endless nightmare full of pain and betrayal and it would take me a very long time to wake up. It would take years.

There I was, out of jail on bail with no hope and not one friend. I had a black eye and a broken nose. I felt broke and ugly. And not one person in this entire world could or did anything to help me in any way at all, except my mother. This is when I truly called on Jesus. And he heard my plea and carried me all the way through.

It still hurts 20 years later, to even think about my family's betrayal. I was already deeply depressed. My father had just died of cancer, and I watched him die a painful death. I had fallen out with my grandmother. A few months prior to that, two of my dogs died. The guy that I thought I was going to marry ended up marrying someone else. My life was so sad and lonely. I was miserable.

I somehow managed to pick myself up. I was studying for my real estate license and in the process of purchasing my second home in the high desert of Southern California. I was an up-and-coming actress, screenwriter, and production coordinator. I had recently caught a 49-pound catfish and a 15-pound trout on a fishing trip with a fisherman that I was in love with, a guy named Chukka. A man whom I thought I would marry. I thought he and I would have been perfect for each other, until he told me that he was going to marry a girl he had recently met.

He had only known the woman for about four months before he married her. He had known me for years and never even mentioned marriage. It was his loss though because his marriage didn't last a year and he spent about $25,000 on that wedding. I was still crushed though. I had also just bought a brand-new SUV which I still have. And until then, I thought I had a super close relationship with my entire family, but I was so wrong. I never would have thought they would all betray me and all of them did. They all betrayed me in one way or another. How could I bounce back from all of that? I really needed a serious vacation from life.

So, as I was being escorted from the courtroom, I looked at the audience. To my surprise and embarrassment, there was everybody that I knew sitting there looking at me as if I was a monster because of what the judge said about me. I understood and appreciated my mother's attempt to show the court that I had support, but it didn't help at all. I just rolled my eyes and shouted, "My life is over!"

That's when I heard my friend Dee say, "No, it's not Meekster."

As I walked out of the courtroom with the half-ounce of dignity that I had left, I briefly asked if I could give my mom my jewelry, a decision I would later regret because my brother stole it and hocked it. Once I left the courtroom and the door closed behind me, I was in another world completely. The next twenty-one months would change my life forever.

Chapter 3

The Other Side of the Door

On the other side of that door was basically a police station. Cops walked around everywhere. The dispatch station sat in the center of the large room. There were jail cells with iron bars and a lot of loud rowdy criminals that were now my neighbors. I was placed in a cell, and I sat down and just started crying.

There was a young woman sitting across from me and she came over to me and put her arms around me and told me that everything was going to be okay. She said at first, she thought I was an attorney until I started crying. I admit, I was wearing a nice outfit, but God must have sent her because her touch soothed me, and I calmed down. At that point, I realized that I had to take a deep breath and deal with it.

I sat in that jail cell for a few hours. I don't know what happened to the young lady. I must have dozed off when they had taken her out. When they came to take me to County Jail, I was called out of the cell and handcuffed by my right wrist with one cuff and the other cuff was attached to the left wrist of a woman named Kai that they had taken from another cell. We were then led to a big black and white Sheriff's bus along with a bunch of handcuffed and chained men.

They let the men board the bus first. I guess that was because there were a lot of them. The men nearly filled the entire bus, even the cage in the back of the bus was full. There were two jump seats in the front of the bus. A cop sat in one seat and a male inmate sat in the other. As I and the other woman boarded the bus, it was like walking on the catwalk. The men on the bus were making all kinds of comments. One said, "You didn't do it, you look innocent." Another said, "You look like Michael Jackson." A few of them asked me to touch their penises. I told those guys, "Maybe later."

This one guy who was seated directly behind me was handsome. We briefly made eye contact as I was seated next to the window. He was handcuffed by his right wrist, so his left hand was free like mine was. As the bus took us on our journey, I looked out the window watching the cars pass by. I placed my elbow on the window and used my arm to brace my head. I started daydreaming about how long it would be before I could drive on the freeway again and how it would be such a long time before I could go fishing again. That's when I felt a hand cupping my left titty. This fool behind me had scooted up closer to me and managed to slip his hand inside of the arm of my blouse.

The first thing I did when I felt his hand on me was look down. Then I looked over my left shoulder and he was right there. Before I could say anything, he started whispering, "Please don't trip, I'm about to be locked up for a long time. They did you wrong girl. They gave me seven years." He kept rubbing my titty. I didn't say anything to get him in trouble. I kind of felt sorry for him, I couldn't imagine doing seven years. And actually, it felt good. I knew it would be a long time before a man would ever touch me again, so I took his whispers as sweet talk. That was one of the naughtiest things that I had ever done, so don't judge me.

For some reason I had accepted my fate and was along for the ride. I wasn't afraid at all. I was heading into unknown terrain with no map. This was a Meekster Adventure for sure. In fact, the night of my arrest, I was online corresponding with people in prison on a site called Prison Pen Pals. Ironically, I wanted to know about prison because I was planning on making a documentary about being in prison.

The trip to County Jail was exciting and miserable. All I could think about was what awaited me. As the cars drove past the bus and people from the cars started waving, things became even more real because I felt helpless, hopeless, and completely restricted from freedom. I couldn't even imagine what it would feel like to have my life and freedom back.

Other people didn't seem to mind because they were repeat offenders, parole violators, or maybe people who were just used to going to jail. However, this was my first time in any kind of trouble, and I was shattered. Little did I know that this was where I needed to be. I desperately needed a vacation from life, and this was it. You can't get further away from life or the real world than this. Thus, began my prison stay-cation. I say stay-cation because I ended up staying longer than I was supposed to.

Chapter 4

Welcome to the Jungle

When the bus arrived at the Twin Towers County Jail, we exited the bus and were escorted inside of the facility. It was complete chaos. It was the loudest environment I had ever been in, and I worked in an ER. Criminals/ inmates are the loudest, most obnoxious beings I have ever seen or heard. They acted worse than wild animals.

Booking: They put men and women in separate holding cells, and they made the men sit on the floor in a tight tripod line. I'm talking penis on your back tight. That was wild to see. After a couple of hours, they pulled me out of the cell and told me to follow the yellow line to another cell. This went on for hours and hours.

Finally, I got to an intake room full of long benches, filled with some of the most undesirable, crunchy women I had ever seen in my life. I had never even seen a scene like this in movies. I mean ho's, junkies, women having withdrawals, women walking around scratching themselves. And they all wanted to talk to me all the time. They never shut up. They kept asking me if I was a lawyer and if I could represent them. I was an inmate just like them. I was just dressed in a nice DK suit, and I looked nicer than everyone in there, including the real lawyers that were there representing their clients. But hey, I take no pride in being the best dressed person in the County Jail. Well, maybe a little, after all, that suit was all I had.

After so many hours they finally called my name and asked me personal information like do you have tattoos? Do you belong to a gang? Do you have AIDS?, etc. Next, they took my fingerprints and palm prints. Then, they gave me a wristband that I would wear for three months until I got to prison, where they would cut it off. The information on the wristband is your name, booking number, your classification, and security level. For instance, Level I was high risk, maximum security. Level II was medium, and Level III was the lowest level of security. Some wristbands told if a person was looking at a life sentence. Those bands had L-WOP (life without parole) on them. Many people hid their wristbands because they didn't want everyone knowing their business. Mine was III, which was very low -level security.

After that, I was totally exhausted and so thirsty. I just wanted to drink some water and lay down. The water was horrible. I had no concept of time, but I know it was the middle of the night or at least it felt like it. I think I followed another line and it led to the chamber of "Budussy" (butt, doo-doo, and pussy is what it smelled like). This is the room where the guards make you take off all your clothes, face the wall, and look down. One by one, they checked our hair and our mouths. Then we had to squat three times and cough. I followed one last blue line to the showers. Then, I was issued my jail clothes, picked up a 2-inch mattress and sheet bundle and headed to my new Pod home.

A Pod is a huge, glass-encased room that houses about fifty super loud women. Some of the Pods were full of small bunk beds and the women used sheets for their privacy. Other Pods had cells as well as bunks. The Pods with cells were high security level Pods. I was placed in a low-level security Pod where mostly everyone who was housed there worked in the kitchen, or as an orderly, or with the janitors. I was escorted into 271 C-Pod, where I would start my new life with my new neighbors or, should I say, roommates.

As soon as I walked in, the women were all over me. They loved my hair and wanted to know all about me. They told me about the jobs to get and schooled me a little. It was so loud in there, it seemed like everyone was talking at once. It was super busy there too. Women were walking around exercising on the second floor where the showers were. Others were playing cards or doing things on their beds.

After about ten minutes, one of the guards opened the Pod door and started asking people if they wanted to work in the kitchen. I said yes, quickly! She looked at my wristband to see what security level I was, and said, "Go get your things and wait here."

As soon as she closed the door, one of the girls that I was talking to named Daysha, told me that I should stay there in that Pod and that I wouldn't like in the other Pod because it was loud, and the girls were rowdy. I thought it can't be louder than this one, but I should have listened to Daysha.

The guard returned and escorted me and a couple of other girls to a different Pod. When I walked into 272 C-Pod, it was much different than the other Pod. There were fewer women in there and most of the beds were upstairs on the second tier. There seemed to be less activity there as well. It was noisy but not as noisy or as busy as the other Pod. The guard didn't tell me anything. She just opened the Pod door and after I walked in, she closed the door behind me. I had no idea what I was supposed to do.

I didn't stop to talk to anyone. I went directly upstairs and looked for an empty bed and put my things on the first empty bunk that I saw. It was an upper bunk and there was a woman on the lower bunk. I made it up and climbed up top. As I looked around the room, I saw rubber boots sitting by the end of people's bunks, but I didn't really think that I needed a pair. I didn't know what I needed. I didn't know anything except that I was exhausted. I had been up for about twenty-eight hours and for the first time since I left court, approximately twenty-two hours prior, I could finally close my eyes and think about what I did to get there. How I ended up in that loud, no clean water having, lights on all night, disco hell.

Sitting on the bed next to me was a young lady who was leaving the next day. She was saying how she couldn't wait to get out so she could hug a tree. I was envious because I wanted to get out and hug a tree. I was hoping with all my might that the judge who sentenced me would have a change of heart and reduce my sentence. I kept that hope alive for as long as I possibly could. After all, hope and prayer were all I had. The young lady next to me just kept talking about leaving and I couldn't wait for her to leave so I could rest.

A couple of beds down from me were a couple who let it be known that they were lovers. They basically had sex the entire few hours that I was there. The worst thing was the noise. But I was finally able to doze off after a few minutes had passed. As soon as I fell asleep, the bed started shaking. There were two women standing at the end of the bed yelling at the woman in the lower bunk. For some bizarre reason, they kept shaking the bed. Not once, not twice, but like five times. It's not easy to shake a metal bed that is secured to the ground, so they must have been doing it on purpose. If they were trying to get my attention, it worked, and it totally pissed me off!

I rose up and asked them nicely, as nicely as I could, "Stop shaking the fucking bed."

The woman on the bottom bunk was a fat stank. She got mad and said, "I ain't shaking the bed. I'm just moving, and I can't help it if I'm big and the bed shakes."

I said, "Well stop moving, because I'm trying to sleep. I'm tired and I would appreciate it if you stopped shaking the bed."

One of her home girls, a fat little roly-poly, got mad at me and said, "Fuck that. If you wanna get down, we can get down. If you don't like noise don't go to jail." Then she started taking off her shirt and told me, "Come on, let's get down." As if she was going to beat me up or something.

I just sat there and looked at her and said, "You know what? I don't even want to fight you." I laid back down. I wasn't scared at all. I was just mentally and physically exhausted. Eventually, they walked away.

I closed my eyes and tried to sleep again. The next thing I knew, a pretty young Mexican lady named Melissa came to my bed and said, "Miss, there's a bed over here by me, get your stuff and go over there."

Without hesitation, I stripped the bed and I followed her to the other side of the room where most of the Mexican women were. I was introduced to a couple of other girls, but I don't remember their names. However, I was very appreciative of Melissa and to this day I owe her and will never forget her. I crawled into bed hoping to just get a little rest and Melissa climbed onto her bed as well, which was right above mine.

She must have seen and heard all the commotion and felt sorry for me. In her own cute little way, she came to rescue me. She was very pretty. I'm guessing that she was around twenty-years-old. She was slim with long, pretty, black hair that she wore in a ponytail. I was tall, 5'7' 145lbs. with locks. It's funny that this little lady came to my rescue. I owe her for life. She had gotten arrested for stealing her father's van and going on a high-speed chase with the cops.

She seemed to know everything that was going on in there. I liked Melissa a lot. I asked her one question before I went to sleep and that was, "What happens if you get into a fight in here?"

She said, "Nothing, but if you're going to fight, do it in the showers."

I said, "Alright thanks, good to know." I felt safe as I laid there on my bunk with Melissa there above me. I knew that I had a friend and I could finally go to sleep.

When I first went to the toilet, I was shocked to see that it was made of metal. I had never seen anything like that before. I later learned that metal kept down the spread of germs. I was also shocked when I saw women walking around naked while I was using the toilet. When I took a shower, I had to be naked in front of everyone. I had a nice body, but I never even stripped naked in PE class in high school. I had to get over that shyness quickly, or else end up with a stomach full of poop and bad body odor.

The "Showers" was the bathroom. It was a huge room with a concrete floor and two showers, two toilets, and two sinks in it, just perfect for fighting (being sarcastic). The guards can't see what is happening in the showers and for some reason, I knew that I would end up fighting those girls in the showers.

Chapter 5

A World Within A World

It felt like as soon as I closed my eyes, the lights came on and they were super bright. The noise was back on too, on high volume and everybody was up scrambling around. I asked Melissa what was happening, and she said people were getting ready to go to their jobs. Most of the women in that Pod worked in the kitchen on different shifts. I heard them call my name over the PA system and Melissa told me to go with her and ask to work in the kitchen so I could have access to extra food. As far as I was concerned, Melissa was my best friend, and I would have done anything she told me to do at that time. In some way, I wonder what would have happened had I asked to work as a porter or something.

I followed Melissa downstairs to a desk where an officer was sitting, passing out job assignments. There was a long line of women, and I was in line behind Melissa. When I approached the officer, I told him my name and he said, "Where are your boots?"

"Boots? I don't have any." I had never been issued any boots.

He said, "You can't work without boots. Go upstairs and get some."

"Uh, I can't just go take somebody's boots. Those girls already don't like me."

"Everything here belongs to the county, so just go upstairs and grab some boots so you can work."

I said, "All right, I tried to tell you." So, I stepped out of line to go back upstairs to get some boots. I think Melissa was standing there waiting for me.

I ran upstairs to get some boots, but I couldn't find any that were my size. I looked over past a bed and I saw a pair of boots that looked like they might fit me. As I walked over to get them and check the size, I felt someone come out of nowhere and push me hard. It was some lady that just came from nowhere. Now that I think about it, she must have been laying on her bed watching me. She probably saw me walk away from fighting those two girls the night before and thought I was a punk or something. I later learned that her name was Tammy Razor.

At first, I thought that she pushed me by accident, so I said, "My bad. I'm just trying to get over there and get those boots."

I tried to walk around her, but she pushed me again, harder. I had never been pushed, especially not like that. I giggled a little because I didn't understand why she was pushing me. I said, "Stop pushing me."

She raised her right hand and said, "You don't know who you're fucking with." I saw that she was holding an orange razor.

Before she could push me a third time, I picked her up, flipped her upside down, and body slammed her onto the concrete floor! I got on top of her and started whaling on her face nonstop. Left, right, left, right, nonstop.

I had blacked out. I had no realization of what was happening. I heard no sound at all. Even though by this time the alarms were going off, and the girls that were there, were on their beds, shouting fighting words of encouragement. I heard nothing at all.

All I could hear was the voice in my head. "Why isn't she fighting back? My hands feel like feathers. I'm not even hurting her." I must have counted ten straight socks to her face. Then, out of my peripheral

20

vision, I saw blood drops and I thought, "Where is that blood coming from? She's not even hitting me back."

All this time, I heard no other sound, nothing at all. And I saw nothing at all. I didn't even see the deputies coming up the stairs and there were a lot of them. They pulled me off her and dragged me to the other side of the room.

I can't even remember if my eyes were open or closed when I was hitting her because I was in such a deep trance. This has never ever happened to me before and it is scary to know that I carry this hidden fighting talent and silent rage. I felt like I had superpower, incredible strength. I would later realize that I had a problem with blackouts. But I never got any help for it. I didn't know where to go to get help for it.

Suddenly, I heard sound again and snapped back to reality. There was an extreme amount of noise going on. The girls were shouting, and the alarms were going off like crazy. There were flashing red and blue lights, like police sirens going off.

The deputy took me to the other side of the room and handcuffed me. I started shouting at him, "I told you this would happen. I told you this would happen." I was crying and I looked toward the stairs and there were so many officers running up the stairs. It was crazy, crazy, crazy and I knew I was in trouble, trouble, trouble. Especially, when I saw them carry Tammy off on a stretcher.

I had been in jail for less than 24 hours and already I was in deep, deep trouble. I didn't realize how much serious trouble I was going to be in. What kind of life is this that I am living now? How did I get here? I mean, when will this madness end? I later learned that the medical staff had to take Tammy to a real hospital, one outside of the jail because the jail hospital didn't have the right equipment to help her in there. She was in pretty bad condition. I really hurt her. But she really asked for it. I mean, she begged for it. Didn't she?

When I got to the bottom of the staircase, the first face I saw looking at me was Melissa. She looked sad for me. I wondered what she was thinking. I wondered if she saw the fight. I paused for a second and looked at her and just shook my head as I was led away by the officer. That would be the last time I saw Melissa for a while. I had no idea what to expect next. My life was in the hands of the jail staff.

I'm sure the girls who wanted to fight me the night before, saw the fight and were glad that I didn't beat them up that way. I honestly never knew that side of me existed. I don't know how I was able to pick that lady up and flip her upside down like that. Whatever came over me or whatever took over me ain't no kind of joke. I felt no anger or evil energy at all. The whole time I was beating her up, I felt peaceful inside. So maybe it was my guardian angel protecting me. There was no rage or anger. As a matter of fact, when Tammy pushed me the first time, I giggled, so I wasn't mad or anything. I was excited to see what working in the kitchen with Melissa was going to be like. I guess I had built up anger that I didn't know about. Or maybe it was built up frustration from all my pain and injustice. I can't even begin to explain or understand why my hearing was muted.

I was taken to a room that looked a little like a visiting room. There were glass windows and lots of metal stools. I was handcuffed by my ankle to one of the metal stools with my wrists still handcuffed behind my back. I was left sitting there for what seemed like hours. I was super agitated. When I would see an officer walk by, I would start shouting at him. They kept ignoring me until I started shouting for a Watch Commander.

I shouted and shouted and shouted at the top of my lungs and would not stop until someone finally came. I'm sure everybody in the whole entire jail could hear me screaming. I felt like I was losing my mind. When the Watch Commander finally came, I tried to explain the whole situation, but he didn't want to hear it. He had already read my initial arrest report and saw the judge's comments and thought I was a monster, too. This situation was basically out of his hands, especially since there had been a medical emergency attached to it. This kind of emergency had never happened in county jail before, not even on the men's side. They were still trying to figure out what to do with me. He was done with me.

I felt like I was in a nightmare and couldn't wake up. I was pretty much on my own and being innocent didn't mean anything. The way he saw it; I was the predator, and Tammy was my victim that I almost killed. I thank God that I didn't kill her. He basically left without even listening to a word I said. And honestly, I was so out of it, I had no concept of what was really happening. It was like I was sleepwalking, but wide awake, if that makes sense. I was basically a walking zombie, and that condition has to have some legality to it.

Fighting and screaming had exhausted me, and I fell asleep. I'm sure everybody in the whole jail was happy that I had stopped screaming. I was awakened by an officer who came to take me to my next destination. I didn't even care where I was going as long as I could rest. I was starting to get used to being led around. It was an adventure into the unknown as far as I saw it.

This time I was led to the bottom of the jail to what felt like a dungeon. And it was a dungeon. It was C-211, a place for the worst of the worst. The worst of the worst? Really? All of this, over a squirrel, $25, and a cell phone. Really?

After what seemed the longest, slowest walk ever, we entered an elevator and went down. When the elevator door opened, there was a very long, dimly lit hallway that looked like it was a mile long. There were red doors on each side of the hallway. As I walked past each room, I saw an information sign with the inmate's last name and offense on it. Each information sign read something different: contraband, insubordinate, fighting, homosecting, etc.

There was a small window in the center of each door. In the lower part of the door was slot about a foot long and six inches wide for food trays to slide though. The creepiest thing about that walk was seeing the faces and eyes looking at me from the small windows as I walked past. They were saying things like, "What you lookin at?" Or "Who you, what you do?"

I thought to myself, they must be crazy, and this must be jail hell. Those women must be really bad. It was cold, stale, and dreary down there. If this didn't earn me jail points, nothing would.

I was starting to feel like I was starring in a scary movie. It's a good movie. It's an exciting, unpredictable movie. But I am ready for this movie to end. Director, please call "Cut." There I was, in the bottom of a dungeon and no one knew where I was. I felt like nobody cared where I was.

My life was very sad, and things were about to get worse. My life was no longer of any value as far as I was concerned. Be very careful of what you ask for in this life because you might just get it. I didn't ask God to send me to jail per say, but I did ask God to send me to another world. I guess things were leading up to this because I did want to see what the inside of jail was like and getting arrested was really the only way to know. Or I could have gotten a job as a correction officer. I never planned on ever being inside of 211 though.

I had been to so many different parts of that jail, I was basically cell hopping, but I had seen enough. This whole experience was more than enough for me. I never ever wanted to go back to that place, never, ever.

Chapter 6

C-211 The Hole

We finally got to my room at the very end of the hallway. It was a corner cell. The guard opened the door and I walked inside. I heard lots of toilets flushing but to my surprise, the room was pretty big. I was still handcuffed so I had to put my wrist through a slot in the door so the officer could remove my handcuffs.

Once I was inside of my room, I felt relieved. There was a sink, a toilet, a bed, and plenty of space. It was about the size of three cells combined. And to my amazement, it was quiet. The quietest part in the whole jail. I felt like I scored big time. This is where they should have taken me from the start. 'The Hole' was actually my favorite part of the jail. I could finally sit down, relax, meditate, and get some much-needed rest. The bed was already made so all I had to do was lay down and close my eyes. And that's exactly what I did.

It had to be about 8am when they took me to the Hole, because I slept for a few hours, and the guard woke me up when she brought me lunch. Meals were the only way to keep track of time there. Lunch was a bologna sandwich and an apple. I don't eat pork so the sandwich did me no good but that was the best apple I ever had. Dinner was something that I had only ever seen in a dog bowl. Some kind of noodles with chunks of spam in it, beans, salad, and a tiny carton of milk. Needless to say, I went to bed starving that night. I sure should have eaten that bologna sandwich because I thought about it all night.

The rest of that evening I exercised. I did sit-ups, push-ups, jumping jacks, and walked in a circle until I was tired. I cleaned the room and for some reason, I laid on the floor, on my back. I looked to my right and under the bed, praise God in Heaven, I found a half of a New Testament Bible. It was like I found gold. I actually found something way better than gold though, I found the word of GOD and that was exactly what I needed.

I started reading the Bible and I didn't stop until the noise started later that night. It seemed like it was a set time every night for the women to start acting out all over the Hole. They were shouting at each other through the opening at the bottom of the doors. This is how they communicated, all night long. I wasn't complaining though. I would take being in the Hole over being in a Pod all day long. I was alone, I had my personal space, and I had my Bible. I was good to go. I figured that I wouldn't be there very long, but I was wrong.

I laid on the floor and put my ear next to the open space at the bottom of the door. I could totally hear their conversations, clearly. They were all shouting at one another, talking major trash. I could even hear them threaten each other. They were making plans to get married once they got to general population or out of jail. It sounded like a madhouse in there. They sounded like demons. This was exciting and scary to me. I listened for a while, until I fell asleep right there on the floor. This form of communication between the inmates would occur every night at the same time. I started to look forward to it.

When I woke up, I didn't know if it was day or night, but the shouting had stopped. I worked out for a while and then picked up the Bible and started reading. As I mentioned before, there were only a few pages and chapters of the New Testament, but it was just what I needed to get by.

Reading the Bible while I was in deep despair would give new meaning in my life. This to me was God's confirmation that I was not alone. That He was with me in my deepest, darkest time of despair. The same as He was always with me throughout my entire life. Reading that Bible brought me back to life. It gave me hope and it brought me peace, something that I had forgotten about. I was ready to live again, and I was ready for whatever came next. I had no fear of anything or anyone at all. I knew that this was my fate and God was leading my path.

The officer came and brought me breakfast. This food looked like food, unlike whatever that was the day before. There were scrambled eggs, a piece of toast, a slice of an orange, and what looked like grits. She also handed me a small carton of milk and an even smaller carton of orange juice. I wasn't complaining. I was too hungry to say anything, except burp. I probably ate that food faster than she could close the slot in the door and lock it. I was looking forward to my bologna sandwich and my apple for lunch. I was disappointed though because that day, they brought me a peanut butter and jelly sandwich and I ate every piece of it.

Later that day, an officer came to my room and told me to go with her. I thought it was time for me to leave the Hole, so I got excited and grabbed my half of a Bible. But the officer told me to leave the Bible there because I would be coming back. I asked where she was taking me, but she didn't answer me. She took me down the long hallway into a small room where there was a lady sitting at a desk. I had never seen this woman before. She looked wild and unkempt, so I knew she was a lawyer.

She introduced herself as my public defender. She said I had been charged with assault and battery against Tammy Razor, the woman I beat up and sent to the hospital.

How was that even possible? She started that fight with me. The lawyer gave me a court date to appear before another judge. She said that I was looking at some serious time for this charge, three years, and a strike on my record. Come to find out, this public pretender was friends with the other public pretender that represented me in the other case. Total conflict of interest but it was hell to prove it. The county must have been mad at me because they had to pay to send Tammy to the hospital.

Absolutely unbelievable. Not one person ever even asked for my side of the story, not even her, and she was my legal representative. Nobody took a statement from me, even though this was clearly self-defense. I knew right then and there that I could give up all hope of getting my original sentence reduced. I was beginning to wonder if I was going to spend the rest of my life in jail. She also told me that I had to register my hands as deadly weapons. Register them with who? I never in my life heard of someone registering their hands as deadly weapons, not even Bruce Lee. They were creating new rules for me. I would get that a lot in the future.

She claimed that I beat the lady so badly that she almost died. She said that they had to take her to an outside hospital because she was unconscious. I didn't know it at the time, but when I picked her up and body slammed her onto the concrete floor, she went semi-unconscious, so all of those socks to her face could have killed her. That is why she wasn't fighting back. Thank God that I did not kill that woman!

I was hoping that the judge in my original case would reduce the 18-month sentence that he imposed on me, once my mother had written to him asking for a sentence reduction. However, after word got back to him about this fight, I could forget about asking him for anything. Especially, since the fight report was wrong. The report said that Tammy Razor was a white woman with blue eyes, when in fact she was black like me. I wonder who wrote that report and why no one proofread it and corrected the mistakes. It didn't seem like I would ever get any kind of break at all.

I felt they were being especially hard on me because I was already in jail for what was considered a violent offense. Nothing I said in my defense mattered. The judicial system is harder on women than they are with men for violent acts. It didn't matter if it was my first time in jail or that I was in there unjustly or that I was defending myself. Nothing even mattered except my complete misery. They won because I was completely miserable and it seemed that there was absolutely nothing that anybody could do to help me, nothing at all. I had nothing. I had nothing at all. God help me!

The walk back to my cell was slow and agonizing. I had so much to think about that I couldn't focus on the girls looking at me through the windows. It didn't even matter. Nothing mattered. I was at the most hopeless point in my life. I had a little luck on my side because things didn't get any worse than that. I mean, what could have really been worse than that? I asked the deputy how long I would be in the Hole, and she said she didn't know. She said that the captain or somebody would let me know how long I would be there soon.

I wasn't even allowed to make a phone call. I couldn't even call my mother to let her know what was going on. I know she was worried about me. I was hoping she was. I needed to believe that someone cared about what was happening to me in there. I needed to believe that, even if it wasn't true. I hope no one ever has to go through what I went through. I don't even want to imagine what the innocent people on Death Row feel like. Once they get you in the jail system, you are not human to them anymore. You are only an inmate with a face and a number. They can do anything they want to you once they lock you up. Your only hope is to have someone on the outside working on your behalf. The only person that can help you once you are incarcerated and placed in the system is God. Oh, and maybe a good lawyer.

Once I got back to my room, I started reading my Bible. I got deep into it and learned about fasting. I decided to fast and hope that God would honor it. For the rest of that day, I exercised and slept until I was awakened for dinner. After eating, I got back in bed and waited for 'The Nightly Shout Show' to start. It was on time as usual.

The next morning, the deputy came to bring me breakfast and I told her that I didn't want it because I was fasting so I could go home. She rolled her eyes and said, "That won't work."

I said, "Yes, it will." I felt confident. I asked to take a shower and she told me yes. The bathroom was a very small room with only one small shower stall. Only one person was allowed out of their cell at a time, so they only needed one shower stall there. The officer stood there and basically watched me wash myself. Women are allowed three showers a week. Men are allowed two showers a week. No wonder the men's side smells. The women's side doesn't smell that great either.

The day went on as usual, with no word about anything pertaining to me being in there. The following day the sergeant came to my room and opened the door. He poked his head inside and said, "Campbell. What happened?"

I told him as best as I could and he said, "Well, they wanted to give you thirty days here, but I'm going to give you twelve."

I replied, "Twelve days in here? You gotta be kidding. She started the fight; I was defending myself. She had a knife."

He said, "She had to go to the hospital and get stitches and that looks bad on your part. Be grateful because I'm cutting you some slack."

I was flabbergasted. But what could I do? I guess the deputy was right, fasting didn't help me go home that day or week or month.

After the sergeant told me how long I would have to be in the Hole, I tried to figure out how I was going to last. I did prefer being in the Hole rather than being in a super loud and busy Pod with a bunch of rowdy women. But the Hole was super lonely. I figured I would work out as much as I could. The Bible only had a few pages to it, so I decided to only read one or two pages a day to help me get through the days. That Bible was my best friend and it brought me peace inside. Before I knew it, I was starting to get used to being there. I certainly wasn't thinking about life on the outside, and to me, that was a good thing.

A few days passed. I had adapted to my environment because I stopped counting the days. The only way for me to pass time was to read. I didn't have a pencil or any paper so I couldn't write any letters or anything. It was boring, very boring. I slept most of the time. My only form of entertainment was 'The Nightly Shout Show'. It was the only thing that I had to look forward to. I was starting to act like the girls in the windows when they looked at me as I walked by. When someone walked past my room, I was at the window looking out at them just like the women were looking out of their window at me when I first arrived there.

The deputy was the only person that I had to talk to. I had to force a conversation with her by constantly asking what was for lunch or dinner. I started to feel the effects of isolation. I still liked it better there than in the Pods. At least I could sleep there. And the noise didn't start until late in the evening. The food was pretty much the same all over the jail. The only complaint I had was not having a pencil and paper so I could write. I didn't get a chance to make one phone call to my mother to let her know I was okay, and I didn't get the opportunity to hire or request my own lawyer. They violated all my rights and at that time there was absolutely nothing that I could do about it.

Chapter 7

A Mother's Love

I had been in the Hole for over a week, and it was really affecting my mental state. I felt numb. One day, the deputy came and opened the meal slot and handed me a letter, it was from my mother. Through all of this, I hadn't cried, not until I read that letter. It was the best thing that happened to me in years. She told me to hang in there as if she sensed what I was going through. I felt her love through the letter, and it touched my soul because for the first time, I felt hopeful.

I broke down and cried until I had no more tears to cry. That letter gave me the only hope that I had. My mother never gave up hope. She never gave up on me. She was out there doing everything that she possibly could to get me out of there. She wrote letters to everyone that she thought would help. She even wrote letters to the governor. May God bless her soul. I had a great mother.

As I was recently going through my memoirs, looking for things to prepare me for writing this book, I found letters that my mother had written to several agencies. One particular letter that she wrote to the judge who originally sentenced me, really got to me. If my mom had been my lawyer back then, I would not be writing this book.

Back then, I saw my situation as a curse. Now, I see it as the big, beautiful blessing that God bestowed on me, and I am forever grateful to God in Heaven. Not only did He give me a good story to tell, but He gave me everything that I asked for, and protected me through it all. All those fights and I walked away without one scratch or bruise. That was a blessing.

One night while I was reading my Bible, 'The Nightly Shout Show' started. I didn't realize it was that time already, but I had an idea. I got on the floor and put my ear to the opening at the bottom of the door and I spoke to the women. I said, "Hey ladies, this is Campbell."

I wasn't shouting, but they heard me. I said, "I've been listening to you guys every night and you need some peace. I want to pray. Will you guys pray with me?" Some of the women were still talking and probably didn't hear me, but one of the women said, "Yes".

As I started to pray. Some women were still talking, but one woman shouted at them and said, "Shut up and let this woman pray for us." And they shut up and let me pray. I thank God for giving me a mother who taught me to believe in God and how to pray to God.

It was beautiful and amazing that the women gave me that much respect. It shows more than anything that all those women had love and respect for God. After I prayed, it felt peaceful there and I could tell that the women felt some peace for the first time in who knows how long. There was calm in the atmosphere that I hadn't felt since I had been there. I prayed for them every night until it was time for me to leave. Those women in C-211 "The Hole" had become my friends.

When my twelve days were up, I left my cell to return to General Population. As I walked down the long hallway, escorted by the deputy, all of the women said, "Good-bye Campbell. Good luck." They saw me through their window as I passed their cells. We had gotten to know each other by name, voice, and prayer and that was special to all of us. I had no idea where I was going next. I knew that I wasn't going home though.

Chapter 8

G-Pop

I was back in General Population. They reprocessed me and gave me a new wristband. The new wristband was blue and white. It had my booking number, my name, and KEEP AWAY on it. There was no more level I, II, III for me. I was marked as bad-ass.

I had to be kept on a certain floor so that I wouldn't run into Tammy Razor again, and this prevented me from working anywhere. The next Pod I was sent to was cool. I got along with everybody. The only thing that I really hated was getting up for count every hour. I didn't have to do that in the Hole; I got up when I was ready, and I went to sleep when I was ready. I didn't have to deal with the cocky deputies either.

Inside of this Pod were mostly cells. There were five bunk beds, but they were taken. There were eight cells on the first floor and eight cells on the second floor, but they were taken too. I had to sleep on the floor atop of a 2-inch yoga mat until either a bed or cell became available. There were only twenty-five women in this Pod, so that was cool. Also, there were five metal tables with metal stools around each table. There were five payphones that surrounded this large pillar at the back of the room.

I had to sleep on the floor for a day or so and then a bed became available. I really didn't mind not having a cell because all the action was in the day-room. Once you were assigned a cell, you had to be locked inside until they unlocked the door. But if you had a bed in the day-room, you could pretty much party all night. We used to play Spades and Dominoes a lot. We had to make the Dominoes from cardboard boxes. We would get newspapers every day and I would always read the fishing reports.

The best thing was the Commissary. Commissary is the jail store. If you had money on your books, you had clout. If you didn't have money on your books, you were issued an indigent kit. The indigent kit consisted of a tiny bar of hotel soap, a half of a toothbrush, a 3-inch tube of toothpaste, and a razor. They were issued once a week. Lucky for me, my mother always made sure that I had money on my books. I could buy anything I wanted.

As the days passed, I began to get to know the girls in the Pod. Surprisingly, a lot of the women already knew who I was. They recognized my voice from the Hole where I used to pray. They knew me from my last name too. I had clout there, I guess. They respected me very much. They gave me anything I wanted. I felt like a Pod Boss. I kind of felt that they were afraid of me. Maybe they saw the fight. Maybe they saw what it said on my wristband. It didn't even matter. Nobody gave me problems, except the deputies.

The deputies were assholes when I first got there. They would raid our Pod during the middle of the night and turn it upside down. They would completely trash the cells and take people's personal belongings. They seemed to enjoy doing this. They would line us up and take us to a gym-sized room, search us, and make us stay there until they were done. We would just sit in the gym and make the best of it. They wouldn't even let us take our cards with us. Most of the time, they didn't find anything. Once in a while they would find cigarettes or contraband during the search. Contraband could be anything from a rubber band made from a rubber glove to the cardboard Dominoes.

They would do this twice a month. The worst part about the raids was when we returned to the Pod and had to clean up the huge mess that they made. That kept us up all night.

The food got better though and that was important. My mom was on it. She told me to request a special diet because I didn't eat pork, and they granted my request with no questions asked. I would get special food served separately from the others. Talk about jealousy. My food would come on a different tray, and it would be hot and good. They even brought me my food first. I didn't even have to line up like the others. I had it going on. My biggest issue was constipation. The only water there came from the sink which was almost too disgusting to drink. They give inmates bottled water now, twenty years later.

I was in 271-F Pod for three months, while I was fighting the new charges. I didn't realize how serious that case with Tammy Razor was. I thought it was just a jailhouse fight. It was much more than that. Had I taken it to trial and lost, and the court found me guilty, I would have been facing seven years in prison.

My mom saw what the system was trying to do to me, so she fired the public pretender and hired a private attorney. My mom was so boss. She walked up to the public pretender after my arraignment and said, "You're fired." It's funny because inmates and the system look at you differently if you have a private attorney. It gives you a higher status. I thank God so much for my mother. She was everything to me. From beginning to end, she was my ace.

When I went to trial for the assault charges against Tammy Razor, I saw Melissa go to the witness stand and I was so happy and surprised to see her! She was there testifying on my behalf. I loved and appreciated her so much. My mom had found her, asked her to help me, and she did. Melissa told the truth. She really had my back. I owe her so much. Now that I'm looking back, Melissa was my angel.

The deputy who sent me up for the boots was there too. He didn't help at all. He said that, when he saw the fight, it looked like I was trying to kill the woman. Finally, they brought Tammy out to take the stand. When I looked at her and saw her face, I felt so bad. I even started crying. She was black all over her face even though she was light skinned. The only thing that was light on her face was a spot on her forehead. It looked like I had broken her entire face. I was surprised that she could even talk. She got on the stand and lied so much. She got caught in several of her lies.

The day of the trial, before the trial started, I asked the judge if I could give him a letter that I had written to him. He said yes and told the bailiff to get the letter from me. He read the entire letter quickly. He then looked at me and didn't say anything. He didn't like me at first, so I was trying my hardest to look as innocent as I could. I was holding my Bible and everything.

During the trial, to everyone's surprise, the judge asked the prosecutor my age. Then he asked her about my criminal history. After she glanced through her papers, she said, "She's 32, Your Honor. She has no history. The judge said, "Most people who are violent don't wait until they are 32 to start showing signs of violence."

He dismissed the case. PRAISE GOD IN HEAVEN! He looked at me and said, "I'm putting you on honorary probation. Young lady, don't get into any more fights." God had put compassion for me in his heart and I was super happy. I smiled so big and said thank you. I held up my Bible and walked out of the courtroom.

Everybody in that courtroom wanted to know what that letter said, especially my attorney, because she basically got paid for doing nothing except being there. To this day, I'm sure that both the prosecutor and my private attorney probably still wonder what my letter said. Well, here it is:

Dear Judge,

I appreciate you for taking the time to read this letter and I pray that it finds you. I would like to ask you to not judge me according to the vicious character that I have been portrayed to be but to look into my eyes and see my heart and judge me according to the woman that you see before you.

I am in no way a monster. And it hurts my soul to know that I have been characterized as one. I love God in Heaven with all my heart and soul, I love my mother with all of my breath, and I have always had a huge respect for the law. I know that everything happened for a reason, even my incarceration, at this point I don't understand why my life has taken such a dramatic turn for the worse nor do I understand why I was taken away from my life so hastily. I do know that God Almighty is in charge and only God knows the outcome of this situation.

Your Honor, please hear my words because I speak them from my heart. I am not an angry, violent person. I have never been in any kind of trouble before in all my 32 years. I love and obey my parents and I am a very productive member of society. I have been wronged and I ask that you hear me. My life before I was incarcerated consisted of me working as a TV commercial and independent film producer. Helping my mother out in every way and fishing at every lake or ocean I could go to with my fiancé. He holds the state record for catching an 89.6lb Catfish out of Irvine Lake. Never in my wildest imagination would I have ever thought I would be in jail, for any reason. I don't drink or do any drugs and was in the process of getting my real estate license.

I say this because no one has represented me for being the God-fearing, respectable person that I am. It is true that I did get into a fight while I was in jail. That was a random series of events gone awry. However, the circumstances were totally fabricated. Please have mercy and compassion in your heart when deciding my fate. I pray that you make your decision justly. I ask you this in the name of my Savior Jesus Christ. He knows that I don't deserve this punishment and I have learned every lesson to be learned.

Thank you.

Sincerely,
Kimeko Campbell

After leaving the courtroom, excited about my victory, reality set in. I was placed back in a holding cell which was the worst. Inside the cell were about fifteen women, either going or coming from court. They were crunchy women, too. Either they were bragging or lying about something. They were all in my business, they even knew that I had a private attorney. There was one toilet with no privacy. Narrow metal benches along the wall so there was no way to get comfortable. I had to sleep sitting up with my back against the wall. We were there all day long from 7am till 4 or 5pm and all they gave us to eat was bologna sandwiches and juice.

This was the part about going to court that I hated most of all. I could have pressed counter charges against Tammy, but I didn't want to go to court again and have to wait in that nasty holding cell ever again.

The bus ride back to County Jail was grueling. Once we were removed from the holding cell, we were handcuffed to another person and shuffled to the big black and white Sheriff's bus again. The front of the bus was full of women and the back of the bus was full of men. Just like the last bus ride, the men were asking for some action.

Most of the women ignored them, but this one Mexican lady didn't. She raised up her shirt and showed them her breasts. One of the guys pulled out his penis and put it up to the separation fence and sure enough she started licking it once the bus took off. I saw this with my own eyes. After she licked it, he didn't want her to lick it anymore, so he asked someone else to do it. Of course, no one else did. I later found out that the Mexican woman who degraded herself was in jail for lewd acts with teenage boys. I was not surprised at all.

Once we got to County Jail, we exited the bus and had to go through processing all over again. We didn't have to go through booking, but we had to sit in another holding cell for a long time. And then we were led to another room and from the smell of it, I knew what that room was. We had to strip and spread our butt cheeks. Then we had to squat and cough three times. After that we were led back to our Pod homes. The reason I keep saying how much I owe Melissa is because she went through all the same things I had gone through, just for me. Just to help me. And she didn't even really know me. No one else would have done that.

When I returned to my Pod and entered my cell, everything that I left was still there. My roommate CeCe was waiting for me to get back. She asked how things went and I told her it was dismissed because of my letter. She was happy for me. CeCe was the sweetest young lady. She was in there for associating with a murder suspect who was her husband. She refused to tell on him, so they arrested her. She wasn't there for too long before they released her. Most of the women were there because of something to do with their boyfriends or husbands. A lot of women that are incarcerated are in for taking the rap for their men. Those women are stupid as far as I'm concerned.

After a couple of months, the women in the Pod had become like a family. We supported each other and kept the Pod peaceful until this one super annoying snitch came into our Pod. She was a serious troublemaker, and she was really manipulative. Almost everybody hated her, even me. She was cool when she first got there, but then she started to show her true colors.

One day I was sitting at the table in the day-room reading the newspaper. When I looked upstairs, I saw four big white girls surrounding the snitch in the corner by the shower and out of the deputy's view. At that time, I didn't know that she was a snitch. I couldn't just sit there and let all of those white girls jump her. I went upstairs and stopped them. I told them that they could fight her one on one but not all at once. They respected me and left her alone. She would later get beaten up by one of them.

By this time, I had been in the County Jail for almost three month and my relationship with the deputies had changed. I was cool with almost all of them. There were a couple of deputies that I liked a lot and could have seen us being friends on the outside. They were sad to see me leave. I really brought a lot of fun, and entertainment to that Pod. I had gotten comfortable, and I was almost afraid to leave. I was apprehensive about going to prison because I didn't know what it would be like. I was tired of being in County Jail though. I had a new, crazy roommate. Her name was Nuney. She was eighteen, Mexican, with long, brown hair, about 5'6" and skinny. She was there for assault.

As soon as she got to our Pod, she took a liking to me and ended up as my cell mate. She had a huge crush on me, but I wasn't interested in her. One night when we were locked in our cell, I was sitting at the desk writing a letter when I heard her softly call my name.

I turned around to see that her arms were covered in blood. She had sliced herself with a razor, because I didn't want to be with her. She wanted my attention and she got it. I cleaned her arms and bandaged her wrists. I didn't want the deputies to see what she did. After that, I was super nice to her because I didn't want her to slice me. As soon as the door was unlocked, I asked the deputy to be moved to another cell, but they didn't move me because I couldn't tell them what happened.

I had to just deal with her for a few more days and I would be taking the Chain to Chowchilla State Prison for Women. I couldn't wait to get away from her. I couldn't wait to see the sun and the moon and breathe fresh air. I had only seen movies or heard stories about prison, so I had no idea what to expect. In my head I was still hoping for an appeal and a new trial, but that didn't happen.

One thing for sure is that we have no control of our lives. We have to let God guide our paths. I didn't know why my life took that turn for what seemed the worst, but I knew that God was with me all of the way and something good would come of it, as long as I stayed focused on the meaning of my life.

At about 3am on October 17, 2002, I heard my name being called over the loudspeaker. "Campbell, get ready to catch the "Chain"." The "Chain" is the bus to prison. They call it the "Chain" because they chain your ankles and wrists, and you have to ride chained up like that all the way there. I didn't have anything to pack up. All I had was paperwork. I gave all my commissary to my crazy bunky Nuney, and I was out of there.

Keep the Faith
by
Kimeko R. Campbell

One thing I know is true
There is no limit to what God can do
My God is never wrong
And when I get weak that's when He is strong.

Whenever you feel alone
You've tried everything and all your hope is gone
This is when God works His best
Because your faith in the Lord is His faithfulness.

So, remember these things
That we must do and say
When our light is gone
God will lead the way.

Without Him we'd fall
And we'd lose the race
So what we've got do
Is hold on to our faith.

God has done so much for me
He opened my eyes when I could not see
One thing that I know for sure
Is when you find Jesus you will need no more.

Chapter 9

The Chain

After breakfast, I said goodbye to the girls of 271-F Pod. I was escorted to another holding cell full of women who were also waiting to take the "Chain". We were each handed a brown paper bag with lunch in it. I was looking forward to a bologna sandwich because I found out that they weren't pork, they were made from turkey, but instead of bologna we got peanut butter and jelly sandwiches. Most of the women had been to prison before. There were only a few first timers, including myself.

After a couple of hours in the holding tank, we were taken outside to board the bus. We remained shackled together the entire trip, even when we went to use the toilet. The good thing was that there were no men on this bus. I was shackled to a Mexican girl named Velda and before I could even sit down, one woman started threatening the woman I was shackled to. She wanted to fight her right then and there. I told the lady, "Look, you're gonna have to go through me to get to her and that ain't gonna happen." I was serious. The lady backed off.

I slept most of the five-hour ride. But when the bus first took off and left the dark underworld of the LA. County Jail, I couldn't stop looking out of the window. I wanted to remind myself of what the city of Downtown Los Angeles looked like because I knew it would be a long time before I would get to see it again. For the first time, I looked at Downtown Los Angeles from a distance and it was actually a beautiful city.

Before I got arrested, I used to see the black and white Sheriff buses and I would sometimes wave to the passengers. Never could I have imagined that I would be on that bus getting waved at. I felt like people could see me through the heavily tinted windows. I was just trippin though. Nobody was probably even looking at me or waving at me.

I just felt like woe is me.

Once we hit the freeway, my third new life's adventure started. We were on our way to the "Big House". I started drifting off, and I saw the mountains and the lakes, and I remembered how I used to enjoy them so much. I wondered if the people I saw at the lake appreciated their freedom. When I was out there on the lake, I didn't think about anything except how fast I could catch a fish and how big the fish was going to be. My biggest thrill was getting new fishing equipment and Teva sandals for my birthday.

I thought about who would be driving my new SUV that I left behind. I wondered if I would have anything left after I was released from prison. I thought about everything, except my family. I didn't want to think about them. I thought about how I hated LA. County Jail. It has to be the nastiest, germ infested, most disgusting place in the world. I was glad that the experience was over. It was time to see what my prison adventure would be like. I just hoped it was going to be somewhat fun.

When we got to our exit at Avenue 22, everybody started to get excited. I was excited! We drove down a long narrow road for a few miles. The road seemed to be leading nowhere. All of sudden, there it was. The entrance to Chowchilla Women's Correctional Facility. It looked more like the entrance to one of the lakes that I had been to or a military base. I don't know what I was expecting, but it wasn't what I saw.

When we pulled inside of the facility, we went through this huge gate. Just like in the movies. There was a guard in the tower holding a rifle and watching us as we drove up. There were warning signs posted everywhere. The signs were warning escapees that the guard would shoot them, and the gates were deadly high voltage risk if touched. Things just got very real. I didn't know what to feel. There was silence on that bus like never before. All the first timers were scared, the returnees felt like they were just going back home. They were making plans before we even got off the bus.

Once we exited the bus, we were ordered to line up against the wall and listen for our names to be called. We were then sent to a holding cell where we were strip searched. After the search, we were issued a muumuu, which is a big grandma dress with flowers on it. We had to wear those muumuus for a week until we were issued our orange CDC prison uniforms.

We were also given a pair of flip flops which were actually shower shoes. We had to wear shoes when we took a shower because the showers were so disgusting that we could catch something with our bare feet. I didn't find out about needing the shower shoes until later, and like an idiot, I sold mine to a lady for two cigarettes the very next day. I had to take a shower with my tennis shoes on until I got some more flip flops.

Next, hey gave us a brown plastic coffee cup, a plastic spoon and fork, a small bottle of shampoo, small tube of toothpaste, and a regular sized toothbrush. I hadn't seen a real toothbrush in three months. The County Jail only issued us travel sized toothbrushes. We waited in the holding tank for about four hours. Then we were called one by one to take a picture for our ID cards and given our prison numbers. I was known as inmate #W-96217.

Finally, we walked across this big grass field. In the center of the field there was a volleyball net and I thought that was super cool because I love playing volleyball. There were also basketball courts. We walked to this big gray stone building that had the number 503 on it in big numbers. There was a black iron door in the center of the building that was controlled by an officer inside of the building. I was about to enter the twilight zone, I thought. What was behind that black iron door? I was about to find out what prison was really like. Ready or not, here I come.

Chapter 10

The Stone Mansion

We went through the door and walked down a short narrow hallway. Inside there were lots of rows of cells. Two levels of cells, and they all had orange, metal, sliding doors. Each door had a long narrow window in the center of it. The window was so narrow that you could hardly see anything out of it

We were all seated in the day-room, where we were oriented. After orientation, we were sent to our cells. Inside of my cell was a metal sink, metal toilet, a metal desk, and a 2-person bunk bed. This cell was smaller than my cell in the County Jail. There was a real mattress on the bed, but this room was simply "Four Walls of Stone". I felt so lost and empty there. There was a woman lying on the top bunk, but she was asleep. I'm glad she was asleep because I really didn't feel like talking. I was tired and uncertain, and I did not like the way that the door slammed behind me. I felt totally confined, almost claustrophobic.

All I could think about was that I had to be there for 18 months. This was worse than jail to me. I hated it. My roommate finally woke up and instructed me on how things went in there. She arrived two days before me and her name was Lisa. She told me that we wouldn't be going out of the room until around 5:00pm, which was dinner-time. After dinner, we had to return to the cell for the rest of the night. I was even more depressed after she told me that.

I couldn't believe that we had to stay in that tiny 6×8 cell for 24 hours. Did they accidentally take me to death row? I later found out that the lower tier, where I was in room 32, went out from 1-4 pm and the upper tier went out from 9am till 12pm. Each tier alternated days so it was fair time for everyone. I was tired, so I did what I did best and that was to sleep.

When dinner was announced, the door clicked and slid open loudly. We stepped out of the cell and waited for the door to close behind us. I had my cup, spoon, and fork in hand. Then we lined up and marched to the chow hall. This is controlled feeding if I ever saw it. It was totally like in every prison movie that I had seen. We had to walk all the way across the big field. The chow hall was a big building, like a school cafeteria, only there were officers flashing their flashlights, directing you when and where to sit, and when to leave.

The first thing I noticed were ice machines. Everything was all right then. I loved ice so much, I couldn't wait to get there just because I knew I would have access to ice. Seriously, I even felt myself smile when I saw the ice machines. I hadn't seen an ice cube in months. And water, oh my goodness, they had filtered water. I drank a lot of it, and it was good. My first meal in prison was chicken breast, black-eyed peas, greens, and cornbread and it was so delicious. I only had about fifteen minutes to eat, but I ate everything on that tray. Lisa even gave me her chicken. She said she didn't like chicken breast. It seemed like forever since I had food like that. After dinner we went directly back to our cells.

I tried to sleep but it was difficult because Lisa kept crying in her sleep. She sounded so sorrowful. I wanted to wake her up and tell her that everything would be all right, but I didn't know if I should or not. The next day I told her that she was crying in her sleep, and she told me that she had bad dreams all of the time. She had been taking psych meds for years, for her severe psychological conditions.

Lisa had a bad childhood. Her father used to rape her and let his friends rape her, too. It started when she was seven-years-old. Her father would beat her and lock her inside of a wooden box for hours to teach her a lesson for crying. He would use objects like hammers, screwdrivers, coat hangers, and bottles to put inside of her. She said that one time, in front of his friends, he made her play with their pet dog's penis. Her mother was never around, but she knew what was going on, as most no good mothers do.

She got married at sixteen to a Sheriff, and he abused her badly too. He set her up so she would go to jail. He planted a gun in her car and followed her. She wouldn't pull over because she was afraid of him. He sounded his siren and called for backup, and they went on a high-speed chase. He wanted custody of their two kids so he could marry her best friend, and move her into their home. Lisa was pissed at her ex-friend, and she had every right to be. She was really angry when her sons wrote to her and told her that her best friend was mistreating them. She had serious revenge in her heart and no matter what I said, she was set on getting revenge. I really couldn't blame her if she did get revenge. Most of the time, I just listened and let her talk. I didn't really have a good story to tell. My life had nothing on hers. We became friends and from then on, I would wake her up whenever I heard her crying in her sleep.

The next day was better. After breakfast, we were walking back to our building when I saw a little bird with a broken wing. It was a baby sparrow. I picked it up and put it in my pocket and took it back to my cell. I named her Cuddles. I didn't even tell Lisa about it. She was leaving the next day so why bother? I kept Cuddles the remainder of the time I was there. I made a bed for her out of a cardboard box from my lunch, and I put a splint on her wing. When it got too cold, I would let her sleep right next to me. I was glad that I found her. She was my little friend and I nursed her back to health. I wish that I could have seen her fly.

After being in the cell for a couple of hours we were allowed to go to the day-room for some recreation. The day-room was large and there was a lot of activity going on. There was a television, two payphones, and a washer and dryer. The women there liked me right away. They even let me hit their rollie's (cigarette). I felt like I could adapt to my new environment.

After a few days, I fell into the routine. It started to feel like this was a normal way of life for me. The women were starting to crush on me, but I didn't want a girlfriend. I wasn't gay, and I was smart enough to not get caught up in any nonsense involving women. Not yet anyway. I was starting to grow weary of being locked in that cell all day. I asked the officers for a job as a porter. There was this one officer, he was cool. His name was Maywood, and he gave me a job as a porter. Being a porter meant that I could stay out of my cell from 9am till 9pm. I liked that job. After working as a porter for three days, I started getting my hustle on.

I would do favors for the girls, and they would pay me later with cigarettes or food. The favors would be passing kites (letters) to other girls on the upper tier or passing lit cigarettes in exchange for cigarettes. I even charged $5 to make three-way phone calls. Only porters were allowed to use the payphones, and people wanted to talk to or send messages to their families.

One day, I found out that making three-way calls was against the rules. The guard station was in the center of the room. It was a big room on the upper level that controlled everything. The guard could see everything that was going on, but there was a slight blind spot.

This one lady named Bertha that I knew from County Jail kept bugging me about making a three-way call to her uncle. I made the call and that was my downfall. I got caught making the call and was fired instantly. I was so mad at her. I made her pay me $25, and she did. I lost my job and that meant that I had to stay in my cell all day long, again. Another thing about losing my job was that I would have to move to another building and figure out how to keep Cuddles hidden.

The next building would be a room with eight women in it. I didn't know how I was going to adjust to being in one room with eight different personalities. That can't be good. The thought didn't excite me at all.

One day, I was lying in bed, and I looked at the wall and I saw how many days I had been there in that cell. I had taken a pencil and marked the wall with a tally mark for each day. I had been there for nineteen days, and I still had two more days to go. It seemed like those last two days took forever.

When the day came for me to move, I was so ready. This whole trip had been a Meekster Adventure and I was on to the next episode. The next episode is always more exciting than the last so stay tuned. I couldn't wait to be able to go outside and feel the sun. I packed up the belongings that I had collected, which consisted of three pairs of orange prison pants, four orange prison shirts, underwear, paperwork, and of course Cuddles, my baby sparrow. I didn't know how my new roommates would react to Cuddles so I was trying to figure out how I was going to keep her. I didn't want to release her to the wild, she might not have survived. I felt the exact same way about Chip, my squirrel.

The day finally came for me to move out of 503 the "Stone Mansion," to a housing unit in building 501, Room 6. At about 10am, I heard the door to my cell click and slide open. It was time for me to go. I used a big, clear, plastic bag to carry my things. I put Cuddles in my pocket, and I was escorted to the next building by an officer named Pile.

On the way there, I asked Officer Pile about the rules regarding animals in the unit. He said he didn't think that it was a good idea for anybody to have pets with so many people in a room. I didn't think so either. I told him that I had a bird in my pocket, and I wanted it to be safe. He didn't believe me until I pulled Cuddles out of my coat pocket. He was shocked. He said he would take her, and give her to a friend who had a bird sanctuary. I was happy about that. At least I knew she would be safe, and that I played a part in her healing process. I love animals.

Chapter 11

A-YARD

When we arrived at the housing unit, there was a huge fence in front of the entrance that had to be unlocked to let us inside. Once inside, I was surprised to see how much of a college dorm it looked like. It didn't seem like prison at all. The other building, 503, was all prison, but this unit felt more like freedom. The day-room was huge. There were ten rows of wooden benches, like church pews, on each side of the room. There were two 40-inch televisions on each side of the room. The women were just chillin' with each other. Some were watching TV, and some were walking around. There were four separate hallways that led to the rooms where the women were housed.

I followed Officer Pile down one of the hallways that led to Room 6, my new home. I noticed that the doors had doorknobs and a large glass window, so no more sliding metal doors. I could actually see who was standing on the other side of the door. Each room had a big window, and you could see into the other rooms clearly. When I got to my room, I thought, *Here I go. What am I going to have to deal with?* The officer used his key to open the door and let me into the room. The doors remained locked at all times, until they were unlocked by an officer who sat in the station, located in the center of the day-room. There was no way to open the door from the inside of the room.

I walked into the room and to my surprise, everyone was very friendly, and I felt very welcomed. I knew one of the women, Lois. She and I had caught the Chain together. She had been to prison six times, mostly for drugs. There were two metal sinks, a shower, and a small, private room with a toilet in it. There were four sets of bunk beds and four sets of lockers, similar to the kind of lockers kids use at school. The bunks were made of metal but for the first time since my incarceration, I had a 5-inch mattress on my bed. It amazed me how eight women could share one room the size of an average master bedroom. I hadn't shared a room with anyone since I was twelve. I had my own apartment at twenty-one, and I never even had a roommate. This was definitely going to test my patience.

The most challenging thing about being in prison, is that you must adapt to your environment very quickly. You have no choice because you never know when you're going to get moved to another room, yard, or institution. It's best to not get attached to anyone or get too comfortable anywhere. It's best to just do your time, find a routine, and stay out of trouble. There are no real friends in prison anyway, mostly just liars and haters. There might be one out of a thousand who actually mean what they say. I made the big mistake of trusting people and I got let down so many times, that I put up my guard. I knew that I wouldn't be the same when I left that place. I just hoped that I wouldn't lose my good qualities.

The first thing I did was take a long hot shower. The water only got so hot, but it was the best shower that I had in months. I felt clean for the first time since I left my apartment and drove to court. I stayed in that shower for half an hour and could have stayed longer. It felt so good. In 503, I had to take my shower in five minutes and the showers sucked. The water pressure was low and there was always someone waiting and watching. Not to mention it was filthy. That long, hot shower, and finding Cuddles a home, gave me life. I was thrilled for the rest of the day.

The women in the room were of different races. There were three black women including myself. There were two Mexican women and three white women. I liked the diversity of the room. I didn't want to be in a room with one race. The women in this room were: Lois who was my black friend from the Chain. Susan was a white girl, she was in there for drugs, Lil Seiz was Mexican, and she used to have seizures all the time. Sophia was Mexican, and she always wore shades. She was cool with me. Then there was Goldie, she was black, and very rowdy and ghetto. My little friend Sleep-A-Lot, was a young, white girl who slept her time away. Then there was Dena, a homeless, older Mexican lady and she snored a lot, very loudly.

After an hour of getting to know my new roommates, they all went to the door. It clicked loudly. Lois opened it and everybody walked out, and I followed them. The doors to all the rooms had been unlocked and all the women were allowed to go outside and program (go outside on your programmed time schedule).

We walked down the hallway toward the day-room and there were about 100 women there waiting for the officer to unlock the gate. The gate remained locked until it was time for the unit to go outside and program. At first, I wondered why the gate had to remain locked, and why the officers were so strict. I learned that this was to prevent other people from other units from sneaking into the building to fight or have sex. If you got caught doing any of those things, you would be considered "Out of Bounds" and lose your yard privileges from 30 to 90 days.

The officer opened the gate, and everybody started rushing out. They couldn't wait to get to the yard and meet up with their friends from other units. They wanted to utilize every second that they could.

Once the women were out, the gate was closed and locked again. The officer unlocked the gate every hour to let women in and out until 3pm (this is called unlock). At 3pm, the yard closed, and the women had to return to their units for body count, mail distribution, and to prepare for dinner which was at 5pm.

A-Yard is where everyone starts out. A lot of the women get transferred to other prisons, rehabilitation programs, or Fire Camps. Others go directly "Over the wall". Over the wall was an expression that people used to refer to the other yards on the other side of a 30-foot wall made of stone. On the other side were B- yard, C-Yard, and D- yard. Those yards had bad, scary reputations, all of them. Over the wall is when you really start doing hard time.

I wanted to go to Fire Camp. I had always wanted to become a firefighter, and I was a perfect candidate since I already had my EMT (Emergency Medical Technician) license. I loved to camp and loved everything about the outdoors. And on top of that, had I gone to Fire Camp, I would have done 35% of my time instead of 50%. That would have taken four months off my time. I wanted to go to any other institution other than where I was. I heard that it was terrible over the wall. Lots of drugs, killings, rapes, just pure hell.

Several days had passed and I managed to find favor with one of the officers in that unit. His name was Officer Davids. He liked me because I was intelligent and smooth. He could tell that I wasn't a troublemaker, so he hired me as a porter. The women in the unit got jealous when I got that second porter job so quickly, because once you get fired from a job, it's unheard of to get another one. A lot of the women had been there longer than me and they couldn't get one job, let alone two. They would tell my boss that I had gotten fired in 503 just so he would fire me, but he didn't. Officer Davids liked me. And I liked him.

After getting familiar with my surroundings, I started hustling again. I would sell cigarettes or get people lights in exchange for something off the canteen list. Canteen is the prison store, and they have everything you need. I hadn't received any money yet, so I needed to hustle. Cigarettes are a hot commodity on A-Yard. Smoking isn't allowed, so people from other yards bring it to A-Yard through the kitchen. Sometimes they would even throw tobacco over the wall. If you got caught smoking on A-Yard, you could get up to 90 days added to your sentence. Most people wanted to smoke when they first got to A-Yard, so I could easily sell one cigarette for $3.

It was easy to get a light once I was on the yard, because I would follow the smoke cloud and track down the smoker. The people who had lit cigarettes would light mine for me, and I would light other people's cigarettes for them as I walked around the track. It was like paying it forward. Just don't get caught smoking. One day I scored three cigarettes and I felt like I was ballin'. That was $9 and I could do a lot with $9 but I wanted to smoke. I couldn't wait to go outside so I could smoke. I had a better chance of smoking outside and not getting busted than I did smoking in my room. The light was easier to get outside too.

The only way we could get a light and smoke in our rooms was to wait until late at night and fish for a light. Fishing was when we would take a string from the elastic part of our panties. We used this string because it expanded into a line, a super thin, long line, like a fishing line. We would tie an unlit rollie (a hand-rolled cigarette) to a ketchup packet to give it weight. And then we would take the ketchup packet and fling it under the door. With the right aim and skill, it would slide across the hallway floor, and slide under the door of the person who had the light.

She would light the rollie and tug on the string, and I would pull in the string and slide the lit rollie under the door into our room. It was just like fishing. I was a pro at it. It was also an incredible sight to see, especially when ten people were fishing at the same time. Sometimes the line would break, and the rollies would be left out there until we could get to them. We would smoke in our rooms and use baby powder to cover the smell. We never got caught.

When it was time for our unit to program, I went outside so I could smoke a cigarette. I smoked my cigarette as I walked. About ten minutes after I had smoked, I ran into Kai, the woman that I was handcuffed to on the bus from court. She was talking to some other women, and showing them her pictures. She recognized me and we hugged and started talking. I didn't know the other women, but there were a few of us standing around, looking at her pictures. None of us were smoking, in fact, I had my last rollie hidden in my bra.

We stood there for a few minutes, when I saw four officers approaching us. They looked like they meant business. They had their hands on their pepper spray canisters and everything. The female officer, named Wallace, pointed to us and said, "You five come over here and hold your hands out."

Before she said that, we had tried to scatter in different directions. I tried to pretend like she wasn't talking to me, so I started to walk away. She said, "You with the dreadlocks, you come too." I had a rollie on me, and I was damn sure that I was not going to get an additional 90 days for having it. I very smoothly reached into my bra to retrieve the rollie, and I put it in my mouth, and swallowed it with every ounce of saliva that I had.

Officer Wallace was super pissed. She yelled, "Open your mouth." I should have opened my mouth and burped in her face. But I didn't dare do that. By the time I opened my mouth, the rollie was in my stomach and that kind of DNA trace evidence hadn't been invented yet. There were hundreds of women out there looking and listening to us, and I think I humiliated her.

She handcuffed me but they let the other women go. Wallace escorted me across the yard in front of everyone. All the other women were on their knees because that was the routine for inmates when there was another inmate being escorted across the yard by an officer.

I was embarrassed at first. Then, all of a sudden, I started feeling proud of myself as I heard women shouting things at me from all across the yard. They were saying things like, "She don't got no evidence, Meko." "Don't talk to her." "Fight it, Meko." I was impressed that so many people knew my name. I had no idea that I was so popular, and I had no idea why. I had only been there a short time and didn't even know anybody at all. But as I was escorted across the yard, and I heard the yells of support from the women, my walk changed from a defeated walk of shame into a cocky George Jefferson strut of pride.

I was impressed with myself for being so popular. They all knew me. They all knew my name, and I had just gotten there. Now I had a reputation for being just as much of a convict as everyone else. As I was being escorted across the yard to the Sergeant's office, I heard someone whisper, "Is that Meko?" From that point on, I knew that I was an official convict. I was just like everyone else, and it was us against them.

As we got closer to the Sergeant's office, reality hit me and I started thinking, "Damn. I'm going to get fired again, and lose my job because of this bs." When we got to the Sergeant's office, Wallace took me into the restroom and tried to use psychology on me. The whole time I was thinking to myself, "Yeah right bitch."

She said, "If you had just been honest with me, you wouldn't be here. I would have let you go."

I was already feeling cocky, so I said, "Whatever, you got nothing on me." I was really beginning to feel and act like a convict, and I enjoyed it. I felt bad-ass.

She strip-searched me and didn't find anything. Then she issued me a 115 citation. This was the first time I had ever heard of a 115 citation, but it wouldn't be the last, not by far. She sent me back to my unit and from the way everybody was gossiping about me, I felt like a movie star. The next day, there were all kinds of rumors going around about what happened to me inside of the Sergeant's office.

Some of the rumors said that the officers beat me up. Some said that they strip-searched me and found tobacco and dope. Some even said that I had a thing going on with Officer Wallace. I was the talk of the yard. It was super amusing to me, because like I said, I did not have a clue that I was so popular. I had only been in prison for about three weeks and for fifteen of those days I was in the administration building. I had actually only been in that housing unit, and on the yard for six days before all of that happened.

When I got back to my room, I received a notice that I was CTQ'd (confined to quarters). This meant that I was confined to my room, and I lost my porter job. I was issued a 115 citation, and I got thirty extra days added to my sentence, plus ninety days loss of yard.

I was heated. I wasn't going to settle for that, so I appealed the charges brought against me on the grounds that there was no evidence and I had witnesses to testify on my behalf. I won the appeal and the charges were dismissed. In the appeal, I demanded that the arresting officer apologize to me because I was traumatized by her unnecessary actions. As a result, she was forced to comply and apologize.

Officer Wallace came to my room the day after she was served with the appeal dismissal notice. She wanted to talk to me. Officers were forbidden to enter any room without probable cause, unless there was an emergency. She actually came inside of the room. She completely broke the rules. She didn't want anyone to hear her apologize so she sent my two roommates out to the day-room. I didn't really trust her because she lied about me. She said that I was smoking when she arrested me. She said that she saw me smoking and that was a lie.

As she walked into the room, I was very smooth. I stepped out as she walked in and pulled the door closed behind me. She was locked in my room. I looked at her through the window in the door and I didn't say anything. She looked at me in disbelief. She was super-heated, and she couldn't do anything about it. She had to wait until unlock to come out of the room which was about ten minutes later. She could have banged on the door or used her radio to call for help. But she too was ashamed to do that because she had broken the rules.

I just walked away and went to the day-room and watched TV, as if nothing ever happened. My roommates asked me where the officer was, and I casually said, "She's down there talking to somebody."

A few minutes later, Officer Wallace came out and spotted me. She had her hand on her pepper spray and she was super angry. She marched up to me, pointed her finger, and yelled, "You, in the game room, now!" Her face was red, and she looked like the devil. For the first time since I had been incarcerated, I was kind of scared. I got up and walked into the game room.

Wallace came in behind me, and locked the door. The other officers were standing by, ready to kick my butt and sound the alarm. She said, "That was unacceptable, and I can send you to Ad-Seg (administration segregation) for what you did. You're out of control, Campbell. I don't know what's wrong with you, an apology is out of the question. I'm sending you to talk to my lieutenant."

Ad-Seg is the Hole for prison. It's in a building similar to 503, but the cells have iron bars instead of sliding doors. Ad-Seg is where the women on death row live. It's a world of its own. People call it jail, and I knew that I didn't want to go there.

When she told me she was sending me to Ad-Seg, I gave in. I started talking to her, and I told her that she used to be my favorite until she lied about me, and tried to set me up to get extra time. And she made me lose my porter job, and that job was all that I had to keep my mind occupied.

She said, "You locked me in your room and didn't have the decency to tell anyone to let me out."

I told her that I was scared. I said I was afraid to tell Swartz to open the door because I didn't want him to beat me up like he beat up Rodney King. True fact: Officer Stacy Swartz (names have been changed) was one of the cops who got fired for beating Rodney King. He went from disgraced police officer to a disgraced correctional officer.

She said, "I used to like you Campbell, but after what you did today, I have my doubts about you."

I said, "That's cold. You know I'm good people."

She said, "I'll tell you what. I'm not apologizing for doing my job, but you tear up that 602 (complaint form) and I'll pretend that nothing happened today, and you'll owe me one."

I said, "Cool. That'll work."

"Off the record," she said, "you swallowed that cigarette, didn't you? I know that you had one."

I looked into her eyes and said, "What cigarette?"

She handed me the 602 and I tore it up. She never said anything else to me after that.

Chapter 12

Hard Time

I couldn't get my porter job back even though I won the appeal and the citation was dismissed. So, once again I was bored and broke. Every night once we were confined to our rooms. My friend Megan from across the hall would ask me to sing and I would. I would put my face to the door and sing through the crack. I would sing the same song every night, *Let's Chill* by Aaron Hall. I would also get different song requests from other women all over the whole unit. But I knew every word of *Let's Chill* so it was my favorite to sing.

One night, I was eating dinner in the chow hall when I saw this object being tossed across the room. It looked like a biscuit and it went from table to table. It would land on one table and the inmates would pick it up and toss it to another table. I didn't know what was going on, but I knew that it was some kind of distraction from the cops (a cop, or police, is what we called the correction officers).

The biscuit landed on my table and bounced to the ground near my foot. It was a package of tobacco that had been sent from another yard. I didn't know that at the time. I waited for a few seconds and then I picked it up and put it in my pants, thinking that no one saw me do that. I got up and discarded my tray, and then I left the chow hall.

On my way back to my unit. This big, Mexican lady with a bald head, covered with tattoos, came up to me and said, "Give me my Clavo." (A Clavo is a package of compressed tobacco). She said that right in front of a cop who was standing there, so she meant business. I didn't know what a Clavo was, but I knew that I had it.

I wasn't scared of her, but I should have been. She was like 6 feet tall, 200 pounds, and she was well known throughout the prison. Her name was Monie and she had connections with everyone, and was not the person to be messed with. I was going to give her the Clavo, but I didn't want to pull it out of my pants in front of people, especially since the cops were out there escorting us to our units. Monie's room was a couple of rooms next to mine, so she could have waited.

Someone told me that I shouldn't give back the Clavo, because I took all the risk by walking out with it and that it was just Monie's bad luck that she didn't catch it. I thought about that, and decided to keep it.

When I got back to my room, there was a whole lot of commotion going on. It was like a madhouse. Everybody from every room in that hall was pointing their finger at me saying, "We know you got it. Give it up." I thought about all the things that I could buy from the canteen with that tobacco. And then I thought that if I started selling cigarettes, they would know for sure that I had it, and I would probably get jumped or stuck with a dirty needle.

Getting jumped didn't frighten me. It was getting stuck with a dirty needle or getting busted selling cigarettes that frightened me. I had just barely escaped going to death row.

I didn't want to keep taking dumb risks. My roommates told me to give it up too. They said it was a bad move. They said that Monie had lots of friends over the wall, and that they were treacherous. They might stick me with a dirty needle or worse. They said that I could get beat up with a lock in a sock. Sophia begged me to give it back. She said that if I didn't give it back that she would have to fight me. And she didn't want me to kick her ass.

I thought about it, and during the next unlock, I went to Monie's room and talked to her. I told her that I would give her the Clavo, but I wanted something in return, because I did take the risk and walk out with it. I wanted three cigarettes, and unlimited lights. She agreed and we hugged on it. We became good friends after that, and peace was restored. Everybody in the whole unit was happy about that, especially Sophia.

Weeks passed and I was still on A-Yard. I was supposed to be there for eight weeks, but it was going on nine weeks, and I was ready to go. It seemed like every other day there was a fight on the yard. I hadn't seen a good fight though. All I saw were chick fights of hair pulling and wild swinging. One day there was a fight in our unit that made me feel on edge. When I saw the girls getting handcuffed, it reminded me of when I got into that fight in the County Jail. I remembered how much trouble I was in at that time and fear hit me for a second, but that fear faded just as quickly as it came.

A few days later, we got two new roommates. Sleep-A-Lot and Dena were gone. One of the new roommates was Velda, the Mexican woman that I protected on the Chain, the other was Holly. Holly was a big, fat, funny, white girl, with mega tattoos all over her arms, and she was also a devil worshiper, and part-time racist. Inside the room, she was really cool and would tell jokes a lot, but she wouldn't even speak to me out on the yard.

One day we were in the room talking, and she told me that she hadn't talked to her mother in years. Her mother was a Christian and didn't approve of her devil worshiping lifestyle, and had disowned her. My mother wrote to me almost every day, and my roommates were jealous. They hardly ever got any mail. I never bragged about my mother writing to me all the time, but I did read some of her letters out loud. I couldn't imagine how it would feel not having my mother in my life.

One day, Holly tried to belittle me by making a comment about me not having any friends who wrote to me. She said that my mother was my only friend on the outs. That struck a nerve with me. Then she made a comment about my religion, because I used to read my Bible, and that was it. I told her that at least I wasn't too far from God for Him to hear my prayers. I said "when God doesn't hear your prayers, you're doomed." I said, "You got all of those devils and demons tattooed all over your body. No wonder your mother doesn't write to you. She is ashamed of you. Your mother probably thinks that she gave birth to the devil. Is your mother's name Rosemary?"

I don't know what part of what I said finally got to her. But she came over to my bed and said, "Get down." she was calling me out, but I didn't realize it yet. I thought that she just wanted to talk to me, because we were cool up to that point. I got down off the bed. I was wearing a huge sweatshirt, and only socks on my feet. I wondered why she put her shoes on before she approached me, but I didn't think twice about it.

I walked over toward the bathroom. She said, "You know what Meko?" and then she swung on me. I was so quick, that I did a boxer move and dodged her punch. I counter-punched her in the face and wrapped her long hair around my hand while I kept punching her in the face. She outweighed me by about 100 pounds, so she tried to use her weight against me. She leaned on me but that didn't stop me from punching her face. She grabbed me and pushed me up against the lockers, and tried to headbutt me, but I headbutted her instead.

My sleeves kept sliding down over my hands and that was her opportunity to hold my arms. I slid across the floor because I was wearing socks. That was the only thing that stopped her from getting knocked out cold. We were both out of breath, but I kept swinging. The women from the other rooms were watching us fight and they were starting to get loud. That was a good fight. At least it was a good fight for me, and nobody stopped it.

I could see that she was hurt, so I stopped hitting her and climbed on my bed before the cops came and we got busted. I looked at her face and she had knots all over it. She jumped into the shower and turned on the water. She was fully clothed in the shower. She looked totally wounded, and I didn't have a scratch on me. My nose was sore, so maybe she did get one punch in. But my nose had been broken before I went to prison, so when I headbutted her, I think I re-injured it.

The next day, I went to the facility doctor for my nose injury, because this was my chance to get some pain pills. I also wanted an ice card so that I could get ice from the chow hall without stealing it. I made up a story about running into the door at night. They didn't believe me, but they didn't have an x-ray machine in the prison. They had to send me to a hospital outside the prison to get an x-ray of my nose. The cops shackled me, and loaded me into the prison van, and took me to the city hospital.

I walked into that hospital all chained up. I was wearing a bright orange prison outfit with big letters on the back that said CDC prisoner. I could hardly walk because of the chains around my ankles. People were staring at me like I was Hannibal Lecter. The way I was all chained up, I felt like him. I had to take little steps. It was embarrassing. Little kids were pointing at me. Mothers were pulling their kids close to them. It was awful.

Once I got to a room, they handcuffed me to a bed and took me to get the x-ray. It didn't show any damage to my nose, but I was there all day.

One of the orderlies came into the room to bring me dinner, and I asked him for some matches and a couple of cigarettes. He said that he didn't smoke, but a few minutes later he brought me a little lighter.

That was so cool of him. The hospital gave me some pain medication, and I had a lighter, so I was winning.

I got back to prison around 8pm, and when I walked into the room, everybody was happy to see me. They thought that I had snitched, and got moved. Holly even came up to me and said, "Meko, I want to talk to you in the bathroom."

I followed her into the bathroom, ready to fight her again, until she said, "Look at what you did to my face." She had two black eyes, and a missing tooth, but to be fair, she had a missing tooth before the fight. I had never given anybody two black eyes before. Maybe my hands were deadly weapons.

I hadn't even looked at her since we fought. She would cover her face at night with her beanie and blanket so that I couldn't see her face. She didn't even go to breakfast for a few days, because she was embarrassed that everybody knew that I beat her up. I would give her my lunch because I felt sorry for her, and I knew she was hungry.

I never told anybody about the lighter, because I didn't trust anyone, and I didn't want to get caught with it and get ninety days, so I sold it for $15 worth of merchandise from canteen. I didn't need that kind of heat on me.

I was out on the yard a few days before I left to go over the wall, and I was sitting next to my friend Megan, who always asked me to sing when we were in our rooms. We were just talking, when all of a sudden, all of the women on the yard started singing *Let's Chill* all at the same time. They were singing to me. I felt so special, I almost cried. Especially when I looked at Monie, and she was smiling at me as she was singing.

The night before I was to leave A-Yard, I was getting my hair twisted by my roommate Goldie. We were having a discussion with Holly about why she worshiped the devil. Holly was pacing as she talked, when suddenly her eyebrows formed an upside-down V.

I thought I was tripping. I said, "How did you do your eyes like that?"

She said, "Like what?" and she kept explaining. I looked at her face and as she was talking, I saw her face transform into an older man's face.

"Stop doing that," I yelled!

Her face changed back. My eyes got wide, and I said, "Stay away from me."

"What did you see?" Holly said.

"I saw the devil. Stay away from me. I ain't playin." Goldie tapped me on the shoulder and said "I saw what you saw Meko." I was on guard after that.

I remember a conversation I had with Holly about our roommate Lil Seiz. Lil Seiz used to have Grand mal seizures all of the time. She also had a lot of money on her books, because she would spend the max on canteen. Whenever she would load up on canteen goods, Holly was her best friend. The maximum she could spend was like $60 but that got you a lot of items and a lot of temporary friends. So, one day I noticed that every time Lil Seiz would have a seizure, and Holly was around.

Holly would run away! I asked Holly why she ran every time she saw Lil Seiz having a seizure without helping her?

She told me that seizures were caused by demons, and she was afraid of the seizure demon because every time it appeared, the hairs on the back of her neck would stand up, and she would be terrified. So she would run away. I guess that is the price you pay for worshiping the devil. He didn't even help her when I was beating her up.

After being on A-Yard for what seemed like an eternity, it was finally time for me to leave. My next adventure would be over the wall to B-Yard. I heard so many bad stories about B-Yard and I'm sure that

B-Yard had heard a lot of stories about me. Ready or not B-Yard, here I come. I can't wait to start my next adventure. I heard my name called over the loudspeaker, telling me to pack up my things and get ready to go "Over the wall". Off to B-Yard I went.

Chapter 13

Over the Wall

When I got to B-Yard, the whole vibe was different. People were smoking freely. They were exercising, and playing volleyball. Some were even listening to music and dancing, not at all what I expected to see. It was like an all-female summer camp. A lot of the women knew me from A-Yard, and they welcomed me. I didn't see the hell part, and I wanted a cigarette. We were allowed to smoke on B-Yard, just not in our rooms. I didn't see anything wrong with B-Yard at all, not yet anyway.

There was also a huge main yard on the other side of B-Yard that you could access by going through a small guard gate. The main yard is where everybody went, especially on the weekends, because it was open until 9pm. It was like going to the park. All the other Yards were allowed out on the main yard except for A-Yard. The main yard was happening, because it was where the drugs and hooch were. Hooch is fermented fruit turned into booze. There were no trees on the main yard. There was only a big wall that women would play handball against or use for shade to hide from the sun.

My new room was in building 506, room 4. When I got inside of the unit, I could tell right away that this was different. People were walking around freely. The door to the day-room remained open. We could come and go as we pleased. There was no huge gate in front of the unit. The doors to the rooms did remain locked, but they were unlocked every hour. I went to my room to unpack my things. It's weird, because I got there with nothing, but over a few months I had accumulated lots of things. I understood why most bums on the street had more than one basket.

I had no idea what to expect with my room. I went inside, and everybody just looked at me. It wasn't a warm feeling at all. No hello's, no how are you, just looks. Surprisingly, I didn't know anybody. The first thing one of them said to me was, "Don't come into my area."

The room was the same as the room on A-Yard. Four sets of bunk beds, eight lockers, two sinks, a shower, and a toilet. I couldn't even look out the window because it was in someone's area. The women in that room were mostly lifers. They called me a transient, because I would be getting moved around the unit.

My bunky was on the bottom bunk, and she was a lifer named Meechie. She was a young black girl, very pretty too. She couldn't have been more than twenty-five years old, if that. She was serving L-WOP (life without parole) for murder. She was in a Crip gang and was in the car when her set did a drive-by shooting. She took the rap, thinking that since she was only sixteen at the time, she would get a break, and her homies would get off. She was wrong. She was nice sometimes, but I never said much to her. I would just listen when she would talk to me, and I never asked too many questions. I knew that according to the prison code of ethics, asking too many questions was a no-go.

I learned that most of the women wanted to talk about themselves. They just wanted to do it at their own pace without being forced to do it. Most of the long termers (ten years or more) and the lifer's had 13-inch televisions. Those little TV's cost $300. They also got the easiest jobs, and I totally understood why. The young lady, whose bed was across from mine, was a thief. A thief is a real bad label to wear in prison. Her name was Baby Girl. She was serving thirty-five years for stabbing her boyfriend to death. She wouldn't tell me all the details, but I could tell by her character that it was a vicious crime.

There was a couple in the corner bunk near the window. Their names were Sarah and Bacardi. They were both young, in their mid-twenties. A nice-looking couple, they were serving life sentences together. And then there were Boxer and Dee. Boxer never told me her story, but she was serving a life sentence. She just said that she was in there because of her drug addiction. I later found out that it was murder. Boxer had killed her girlfriend, and decapitated her all because she was jealous. She thought that her girlfriend was leaving her for a man. Dee had been down for fourteen years. She was going home in five months, and she was very happy. The last one was Shay. She was in for violating her parole. She was leaving in two months. Lucky her. I still had thirteen months left.

It felt creepy and strange sleeping in a room with a bunch of murderers, especially when they all had attitudes. They never offered me any of the food they cooked, and they made me feel very uncomfortable. I would go out of the room whenever I had a chance. I would stay out for as long as I possibly could. That room was gray and gloomy. They didn't like me at first because they knew that I would be going home, and that room would be their home for the rest of their lives. I felt sorry for them. They actually told me why they were so distant with me. They had a rule: Don't get attached to anyone, because you never know when that person is going to leave or where they will go.

I must say that B-Yard was much more relaxed than A-Yard. Everybody was smoking, and almost everybody had lighters. There were these light boxes in front of the units. So, people could light their cigarettes if they didn't have a lighter. Sometimes I would use batteries to light my cigarette because I didn't have a lighter, and I wasn't going to pay $15 for one. Besides, I liked using batteries, it made me feel like a real convict. One cool thing about the room that I was in was that it was a smoking room. At night when the doors were locked, we would smoke.

I started getting along with the girls in my room after a few days. I was getting the routine down, which was to basically keep the room clean. If it wasn't my day to clean, I had to leave the room by 9am so the other person could clean and have some time to herself. That was cool, but some days I didn't want to get up at 9 am and leave.

Eventually, that would become a problem. I felt that if I was on my bed and out of the way, it shouldn't be a problem with me sleeping in. Whenever I would sleep in on someone else's day to clean, they would play their music really loud and make a lot of noise. I must have heard that song *Beautiful* by Snoop a thousand times. They would play that song every day. I despise that song.

Eventually I would give in, and would leave the room. I had to look at it from their perspective. It was their home for the rest of their lives, and I was just passing through. I went by their rules and didn't give them any problems. After my first week in that room, the women started to like me, and even included me into their conversations. Meechie even let me sit on her bed and watch television, which was cool. Bacardi let me borrow some of her clothes. I was still wearing the orange prison CDC uniform, because I hadn't received my box yet. My mother had sent me a box of things that were allowed, such as shoes, clothes, underwear, perfume, pajamas, sunglasses, a Walkman, cassettes, and CDs.

We were allowed one box every three months.

The day came when it was my turn to go shopping for food and hygiene supplies. I had $80 on my books, and I had planned to spend every dime. After I loaded up my huge clear plastic bag with goodies, I walked back to my unit. Women that I had never seen before swarmed around me, and started asking me for my stuff. People in prison had no problem begging.

When I got back to my room, Meechie confronted me. She started calling me a snitch because of some lie that this girl from County Jail told her about me. I was ready to fight her just for calling me a snitch with no proof. She must have thought about it, because she backed off and left me alone. People won't pick a fight with you if they don't see any fear in you. I never showed any fear to anyone because I wasn't afraid of anyone, especially not her. I always kept in mind that those women were lifers, and had nothing to lose. I had everything to lose.

One evening, I decided to go outside for a walk and get some fresh air. Things felt strange out there. People were arguing and getting loud. This black lady was walking across the yard talking big trash to a Mexican lady. I sat on the grass in front of my unit and watched. I could feel that something was about to happen. After about two minutes they all started fighting. I mean all the women on the yard were fighting. It was a riot. Mexicans were fighting other Mexicans. Blacks were fighting blacks and Mexicans. White girls were in the mix too. Some of the women were trying to stop it, but it just kept getting bigger and bigger. There were about twenty women out there fighting.

I walked to my unit and tried to go inside but it was too late. The alarm had sounded. The cops were out in riot gear and had stormed the yard. They came in like a SWAT team. The cops made everyone get down. I was scared because the cops were handcuffing and pepper spraying everyone out there. I was so glad that I had walked away when I did, because I was near the unit and not the yard, so I didn't get into trouble.

After the cops had handcuffed the women involved in the riot, they made everyone else who was outside stand in a single file. One by one they checked our arms and faces for marks and bruises to see if we were involved. After they cleared everyone in line, they sent us back to our units. The whole yard, every unit was put on lock-down for two weeks. This meant that I had to stay in my murderer-infested room for two whole weeks. No day-room, no yard, no nothing. The only time we were allowed out of the room was for breakfast and dinner. We couldn't even go outside and smoke.

I sank into a depression. I was finally feeling like I was in prison. Most of the days on lock-down, I would write poems or letters to my mother. I wouldn't tell her how I was really feeling because I didn't want her to worry more than she already was. I knew that she could feel my sadness through the ink. I felt sad and alone, and I had so much more time left. It was only February and I had to be there until March of the following year. I didn't know how I was going to make it through without getting into more trouble. I knew that I would be tested by quite a few more people before my time was up. I put my guard up and I did what I had to do, which was to deal with whatever came my way, one day at a time. I kind of felt like a little girl because I wanted my momma.

After two long grueling weeks of being confined to our room, we were finally released from lock-down. The warden put word out that if there was another riot, we would be put on lock-down indefinitely. I was just tired. Tired of being locked down. Tired of the fighting. Tired of the women. Just tired and I wanted to go home. I missed my life. I missed the things that I had and didn't appreciate. I missed my freedom so much.

I had no choice but to deal with it all as best as I could. I kept in my mind that "This Too Shall Pass" and that seemed to get me through. I also saw how other women were in there for the rest of their lives, and that would make anybody want to die. Just the thought of having to sleep on those iron beds for the rest of your life is torture. Everything you own has to be kept in one locker. At any given time, the cops can take what you have. Your only comfort is a 13-inch television to look at and maybe a radio to listen to. Pure torture. Like that theme song from the television show Beretta: *Don't do the crime if you can't to the time, no, no, no, don't do it.*

How could I have complained about being unjustly sentenced to eighteen months when a lot of those women were serving life? A lot of the young girls were doing time because they took the rap for someone else. I wouldn't go to jail and serve a life sentence for nobody. I wouldn't let anybody take the rap, and go to jail for life for something that I did either.

I had been on B-Yard for two weeks and I was finally assigned a counselor for job assistance. They had a Fire Camp program hat I wanted join. The women got to live in a fire station located in the open woods. That's where I wanted to be with all my heart. I knew that I could take that firefighting experience to the outside world with me. I really wanted to be a firefighter, even before I went to jail.

Besides, I saw no legitimate reason for them to have kept me there in prison. There was no way for me to be productive. In fact, the thought of being in one of the toughest prisons in America really made me wonder what would become of me. I questioned my future, because it didn't seem certain. I was told that if I went to Fire Camp, everything would be different. The program was located at another prison, and that prison was more like a college campus and not so much like the Bronx projects. I put in a request to join the program and waited to hear back.

Everybody at Chowchilla was hard and angry. They only wanted to use and abuse people. I saw it first hand when my roommate Baby Girl kept begging for my stuff. At first, I gave her some tobacco, and then I let her use my mayonnaise. Then she tried to use me, so I stopped giving her anything. I didn't feel sorry for her anymore. I wasn't giving anything away anymore, unless I wanted to. I had been warned on A-Yard about letting people take advantage of me and about people trying to "Take My Day," which meant that someone would purposely pick a fight with you or plant something on you so you could lose your day to parole. Holly on A-Yard tried to take my day. I was skeptical of everyone. I hadn't made any friends either, only canteen friends.

When I first got to B-yard, I didn't have anything. My money hadn't transferred yet and I had to use indigent kits. There was a little white lady named Krissy who tried to be my friend. One day I told her that I needed soap to wash my clothes, and later that day she brought me a big can of soap powder. I appreciated that and I would walk with her from time to time. One day, I was out on the yard and this rough looking white girl named Robin told me not to talk to Krissy, because she was a baby killer!

Chapter 14

Her Story

I told Robin to mind her own business. She couldn't tell me who to talk to. Krissy helped me when nobody else did, and I wasn't going to stop talking to her just because she said so.

Krissy looked like a child herself, she was barely five feet tall and very young, and she seemed sweet. The next time I saw Krissy, she wanted to show me some pictures. As we were looking through the pictures, I noticed that she had pictures of her son as he was growing but the pictures of her daughter remained at the same age. Her son was about nine-years-old, and her daughter was about two-years-old. I didn't see any pictures of her daughter growing up. I asked her what happened to her daughter, and why her daughter's pictures stopped. I looked into her eyes, and told her to tell me her story.

She told me that she didn't kill her daughter and that her abusive husband did and framed her. She said that he would beat her, and his family wouldn't even stop him from beating her when they saw him doing it. One of his relatives was a cop and he never got arrested. She said that she tried to leave several times, and would even run out into the dark woods with no shoes on to hide from him. She would get too cold and go back because she had nowhere to go.

She told me that one night her daughter kept crying and her husband was getting mad. He made a bottle for the baby, and told her to give it to her. A short time later the daughter was on the toilet, leaned forward, and fell to the floor. The husband ran cold water and put the baby in the tub, but she wouldn't wake up. They called the ambulance, and the baby was taken to the hospital. A few days later the baby died. The autopsy said that she died from salt poisoning. Her husband denied making the bottle and was never charged. She received life with the possibility of parole after twenty-five years.

Her story sounded logical. I wasn't going to judge her. Whether she did it or not, she was paying the price for it, and living in that hell hole for 25 years was a price to pay.

I was still broke. I knew there had to be a hustle for me but just didn't know what. Luckily, I saw Velda walking on the yard. Velda is the woman on the bus who I prevented from getting beat up. I didn't do it for her. I did it because I was not about to get pepper sprayed while I was handcuffed on the bus. I hadn't seen her since A-Yard, and she owed me $60. Perfect timing. She was just who I wanted to see.

She owed me $60 for stealing my stamps on A-Yard when she moved into my room. She stole them and tried to hide them, but one of my roommates found them. The whole room was very angry with her. They were angrier than I was. They urinated in her shoes and wet her clothes, and threatened to beat her up. They told me that it was my call. I felt sorry for her and told them to let her be. I didn't want anybody to get in trouble over stamps. She was moved from the room that same night.

When she saw me, she told me that she was going to pay me right away. And she did. I had enough supplies to get me through until my money came. I bought lots of tobacco and coffee because I could always sell that at the end of the month. Everybody would run out and start craving it. I even sold ramen noodles. I also wrote personal poems for people. I had started to like the room. I got along with everybody, even the young couple, but it was time for me to move on.

My next room sucked! I hated everybody in it, especially this one dyke named Dickhead. Lesbian dykes were called boys because that was the closest to a man that the girls could get. The second I moved into the room, I knew that Dickhead and I were going to have it out!

Dickhead was jealous of me because I would hang with Kai on A-Yard, and she was in love with Kai. I didn't even like Kai, but I used to pretend that I did to make Dickhead jealous. I didn't like her at all. She talked too much and had this thick, awful, Cuban accent. One time I was asleep, and she woke me up to ask me if I cleaned the room. She would say, "Lady, did chu clen?"

I told her not to touch me anymore or I would kick her ass. I told her not to talk to me anymore or I would kick her ass. I told her that if she woke me up again, I was going to fuck her up. I was serious about it. I told her that I didn't clean and that was that.

A few days passed and I grew to hate that room more. They would get up at 6am and start cleaning and making all kinds of noise. I would just lay there all day to piss them off. I didn't lift a finger to help.

This one night, I was really angry with the entire room, so I got up at around 2am and started cleaning the room. Dickhead got in my face and before she could say a word, I thumped her hard in the nose. She held her nose and called me a bitch. I pushed her into my bunky's locker and my bunky woke up. A cop came to the door and asked what was going on, and we said that we were cleaning. Two days later, I got moved into another room. I was glad because I was going to give her a black eye if I stayed.

The next room was down another hall, and it was cool from the start. It was mostly black, and everybody had lighters. In the last room, nobody would give me a light so I wouldn't smoke because I wasn't going to ask them for anything. The new room was different. The women in that room liked me from the start. They would ask me so many questions. They wanted to know if I was a boy or a girl. The title boy or girl is how people identified gay people. I wasn't gay. I had a couple of experiences with women when I was younger, but no girlfriends or wives. Actually, I was in love with a man before I was arrested.

Ceze said, "I can picture you in a dress so you're not a boy, but you don't wear makeup so you're not a girly girl."

I said, "I'm just me. I'm not going to pretend to be a boy. I'm proud to be a woman." I never wore makeup because I never needed to. Ceze, the one who had been there the longest, explained everything about "The Game," and I made the choice to be a "Boy." Ceze said that everybody in that institution was pretty much gay, so even if you say that you're straight, people will want you more. This is why women got "Turned out!".

I thought it would have been stupid for me to be a girl. The "Girls" did everything for the "Boys." The girls cooked and cleaned. They bought their boyfriends clothes, shoes, radios, etc. They ironed their clothes. And would even have their family send boxes to their boyfriends. All the boys had to do was occasionally call their girl a bitch and spit. Once I got over the feeling of disrespecting women, I was Ceze's protégé.

Ceze had been down for ten years for pimping and pandering. Her story was that she was a Madam, like Heidi Fleiss, and she got caught. That's it. She was getting paroled in a few months, so she was chilled out. When I first met her, she gave off a pimp vibe. She was smooth like jazz and up on everything. She knew everything about everybody. She knew all about me before I walked in the room, and she could read me like a book. She liked me from the start, and I liked her.

Once I had established my identity as a boy, I never had to spit or call anybody a bitch, except another boy. All I really had to do was sit in the day-room and talk to women. Or I would dress nice and go to the yard. I had received my clothes by then. I had Levi's 501 jeans, white T-shirts, sunglasses, white K-Swiss tennis shoes. I was the sexiest and the best-looking boy in the whole prison. I had major SWAG. I got everything that I needed. So many women wanted to be with me that it was a turn off. All the attention showed me just how desperate and lonely the women were.

Ceze was my mentor. She gave me my first mission with a girl. It was a white girl, and her grill was burnt. I couldn't stand to look at her, and she always wanted to be up under me. When she would sit next to me, I would get up and leave. Ceze said that I had to kick it with that girl for a month, but I couldn't do it. Not even for a box full of goodies. One day, the lady asked me for a kiss and that was it. I was done. I gave her my time and that was all that she was going to get from me.

The next lady that I was to use was a white girl named Chamberlin. She was a thick, tall, corn-fed lady and she was really after me. I made the mistake of saying hi to her one day, and she wouldn't stop following me after that. One time I was talking to her, and I looked at her teeth and thought, *at least she has teeth.* If I was going to be interested in anyone, they would have to have nice teeth and a pretty face. I let her cook for me a few times. We were talking one day; I looked at her mouth, and noticed her tooth was missing in the front. It freaked me out. She caught me staring at her mouth and realized that she had forgotten to put her fake tooth back in. I was done after that.

The problem with Chamberlin was that she kept stalking me. I did everything that I could to get her to hate me, but it made her like me even more. One day we were playing Spades and she was my partner. She put her foot on top of mine under the table and I stomped on it!

Later that same evening my friend Melissa moved into my unit. I was hoping that I would see her again. I was so happy that I finally had a real friend there, and couldn't wait to catch up. I hadn't seen Melissa since we were in court for my case against Tammy Razor.

I told Melissa to pretend that she was my girlfriend so that Chamberlin would leave me alone, and it worked. That was all it took. Chamberlin left me alone. Melissa was like my little sister there. We had each other's backs. I would have lost my day to go home over Melissa, and I almost did over a boy named Reno.

One afternoon, I was talking with Melissa in the day-room. She put her leg over mine and we were just chilling. All of a sudden, this boy named Reno walked up to us and looked at Melissa like she had a problem with her. Melissa got up and went to talk to her, and then came and sat back down next to me. Reno didn't say a word to me. She just mad dogged me and walked off. After that, I put Reno on my "Fuck people up list".

My food and tobacco supply was getting low so Ceze said to me in her low-pitched pimp voice, "Girl, you don't need your mother to send you no money. Just keep letting these bitches supply you with everything you need. You won't have to spend a dime of your money if you play these Ho's right." Ceze was right, but the problem was that I was already tired of those Ho's, and I wasn't a pimp kind of person. I learned though, and I learned quickly.

I would play the white girls because they were easy to get. They had all the money, and they seemed to be happy being my Ho's. I couldn't bring myself to use black or Mexican women. I would end up giving them things. I guess that I was a part-time pimp. After all these years, I finally realized that Ceze was pimping me all along. Now that I think about it, whenever I would score goodies from the women that she set me up with, I would give her something. Wow. Ceze was a smooth criminal. She was grooming me the whole time. I'm not mad at her. She groomed me well.

I never had to kiss anyone or do anything other than sit with them in the day-room and occasionally say, "Where's my stuff?" I didn't even have to walk on the yard with any of them. The last woman I can remember using was an older Colombian woman named Patricia. She was classy and had big money. Patricia was serving time for embezzlement. She would send me messages telling me how much she admired me. She was much older than me, so I thought it would be harder to get things from her. Turned out, it was easier. I didn't even have to ask her for anything. She just gave it to me. One morning, Patricia came to my room with a huge bagful of goodies, full to the brim. Ceze just looked at me and smiled all proud like.

A few days after Patricia gave me that bag of goodies, she started acting as if she was my girlfriend. She would be at my window watching me sleep. Creepy. I would open my eyes and she would be right there, staring at me through the window. What finally did it for me was when she told me that she had changed her work hours so she could spend more time with me. I told her that I didn't like the way that she was acting, and she got mad at me and started saying all the things that she had done for me in front of everyone. I checked her right then and there. When I got back to my room, the first thing that Ceze said was, "Shake her." And I did.

My other roommates weren't as involved with my personal life as Ceze was. They liked me though. My roommate Eddy had been down for three years for child negligence. Her story was that she let her Pit Bull Terrier dog gnaw her seven-year-old son to death while she watched. She claimed she couldn't control the dog. And she couldn't stop the dog from attacking her son. She was sentenced to seven years. I kind of feel as though she did it on purpose, because she had a dark, ugly, spirit and nobody really liked her. She never received mail from anyone. At first, I left sorry for her but then I found out that she was evil, and that her family had disowned her.

There was a woman named Mohamed in the room. Her bed was next to the wall across from mine. She was a killer. She was serving ten years and had six years left. She liked me a lot, but I let it be known that I didn't like her for anything other than an associate. I was very leery of her, especially once I found out that she had no remorse at all for what she had done. Mohamad joked as she told me her story. She said that she had stabbed a man seventeen times and slapped him so hard across his face that she left her hand print. That hand print is what got her convicted.

The man that she killed was a drug dealer and so was she. One night, the deal went bad, and the man put a gun to her six-year-old son's head, and demanded the dope and money that she had stolen from him. He didn't kill her son because she gave him the dope and money back. A few days later, Mohamed and her crew went and shot the man's family up and robbed them. The man who had put the gun to her son's head tried to run. But she stabbed him in the back and kept stabbing him until the knife broke. Then she turned him over and slapped him so hard that she left her hand print. After she told me her story, I was speechless. She was laughing.

One day, I came out of the bathroom to find Mohamed sitting on my bed naked. I told her to get out of my bed and I was serious. She was embarrassed. I don't know what she expected to happen or why would she even think that. My motto was to never get involved with a roommate. I would use that as an excuse to not hurt anyone's feelings. She wasn't ugly and she had nice body, but she was a psycho killer, and I wasn't gay. I was just acting.

Chapter 15

Fire Camp Blues

After being on B- yard for three months, I was getting tired of being there. I had three people on my "Fuck people up list", and I was feeling the urge to mark them off. I had started going to school, not by choice, but because my counselor denied my entrance into Fire Camp. I was so angry. I had a college degree and she placed me in a GED class. I despised her so much. I appealed her denial all the way to the Supreme Court of Chowchilla State Prison. I kept writing the officials four-page handwritten letters demanding to go to Fire Camp. I kept appealing and writing until I was heard by a panel of prison officials.

There I was at a huge round table that sat at least ten people. All the officials were present, dressed in their suits and ties. I sat there in my T-shirt and jeans demanding to know why I couldn't go to Fire Camp. I addressed each one of them and they tried to explain, but I didn't hear a word they said after they refused me. I would not let that meeting end. I was just about to pull my race card. But my counselor pulled out a 115 citation that I had just gotten two days prior to that meeting, for some dumb shit. I wanted to gnaw on her. I argued that too!

I had gotten a 115 for stealing a Michael Jackson cassette tape from class, and I got busted trying to bring it in through the work change station. I told the panel that it was my counselor's fault. She had no reason to send me to a GED class when I had a college degree.

I told them that I got bored in that class and I wanted the attention of someone higher up in rank. It was a good argument, but I was still denied. Instead of Fire Camp they sent me to C-Yard to work on an Almond Farm. I just could not escape my fate.

I was more than ready to leave B-Yard, especially since Melissa had left. She got transferred to D-yard. I decided to work on my "Fuck people up list". When Reno walked into the day-room. I wanted to fuck her up just because she reminded me of Melissa. I kind of knew Reno from A-Yard. She was in the room across from mine. She looked just like a boy, talked like a boy, and walked like a boy. She believed that she really was a boy. When we were on A-Yard, I was in my room one day and I looked into Reno's room. I saw what looked like some girls playing in a hammock made from sheets. They looked like they were having fun. An hour later, the cops swarmed their room, and they took Reno and three other women out in handcuffs.

One of the girls in the room that night, filed charges against Reno for rape. The girl said that Reno had held her down and fondled her and told her that now she knew what it felt like to be in prison. They all went to jail. I actually felt sorry for Reno, especially after she told me her story. Reno's mother had died the previous December, and she was still grieving. She had a very sad background. I knew that all she really wanted was for someone to love her, as do we all.

Reno had been raped by her brother's friend. During the rape, he used the barrel of a shotgun to penetrate her. She got pregnant and her brother found out about it and killed his friend. That same brother was killed in a drive-by shooting a few days later. He died in her arms. She was homeless and wandered the streets when she got arrested for a parole violation. She was only twenty-one, but that was her third time being in prison. At times, Reno was suicidal. Prison life was all that she had known. I felt sorry for her and put a mark by her name on my list. I didn't remove her name, but I put a mark by it, just in case.

Reno would later ask me to testify for her about the rape charges that she was facing. She was looking at four to seven years for that. I told her to fuck off, and not get me or Melissa involved in that mess. And that was that. I was not in that room when it happened, and didn't want anything to do with her or her situation. I just wanted to know her story.

I had been on B-Yard for 5 months and wondered how I managed to stay away from getting into any fights. It was a miracle. I had five people on my "fuck people up" list and things were getting hectic in my unit. I still had issues with Dickhead. We almost got into a fight in the day-room, because I told her that her new haircut made her head look like a real penis. Ceze had a girlfriend who was jealous of our friendship. I think Ceze really wanted to see me fight her girlfriend, because she used to instigate in her own way. Some other chick wanted to fight me, but I can't remember why. And then there was Scrappy.

Scrappy was like a yard dog, and she looked like one too. She was a black girl and she looked like a catfish. She had a Mexican girlfriend named Tracy and together they were a terror team. They were always getting into fights with people. They thought that they were the baddest bitches on B-Yard. And I wanted to fight both of them. I wanted to fight Scrappy when I first got to B-Yard. She had it out for me from the beginning, and I wanted to show her who was boss. Tracy didn't want anything to do with me. She knew that I would snap her in two.

Scrappy was serving a seven-year sentence for forgery. She almost got fifteen years, but she took a plea deal. She didn't appreciate the blessing that she had received. Each fight that you got into on the yard would earn you 90 to 120 extra days. She had already lost a year from fighting, and had been to jail many times. And so did Tracy.

One night, I was standing outside of the unit smoking with my friend, when Scrappy called me out. She was talking major crap in front of everyone. Even Ceze was out there watching from the shadows. I looked at Scrappy and said, "Ugly people always want to fight, because they have nothing to lose."

She got mad and called me a bitch. I was so cool and smooth. I took a puff of my cigarette and blew the smoke in her face. She got so angry that she acted like her friend was holding her back from fighting me. I told her friend to let her go. But she didn't. Instead, they walked off.

A cop was standing there just watching the whole thing. Later, that same cop came up to me and asked me why everybody was always mad at me. I told her it was simple – they were jealous. I saw Scrappy in the day-room a few minutes later and I told her to come to my room at unlock so we could do the damn thing. I went to my room and waited but she never showed up. She never said anything else to me after that. I didn't have any more problems after that incident.

July 12, 2003 was my last day on B-Yard. After I had gotten to know everyone and had gotten semi-comfortable, it was time to move on to the next Meekster Adventure, where each episode was just as exciting as the last. Only God knew what was coming next. Ready or not C-Yard, here I come.

SNAKES
By
Kimeko R. Campbell

I close my eyes and I dream about snakes
I see them move I even hear the sounds they make
Sometimes they are all around me or in the distance up ahead
One time there were two of them wrapped around my hand

I try to weed out people
To see who the snakes represent
But it seems that there's just too many
Snakes in the pit

Over and over and over again
I look at my friends and see the serpents within
The closer they get the more danger I'm in
Just laying and waiting to strike at me again

I know that one day I'm going to get bit
If I don't watch out and climb out of this pit
The next time I dream about snakes I know what I'll do
I'll grab it by the head and I'll snap it in two

When I wake up, I'll tell my so-called friends
Get behind me Satan your treachery has come to an end
GOD is on my side, and no one can do me harm
The Lord is my shield, my strength and good luck charm

The Lord is also my Shepherd
And He's guiding every step I take
I will soon dream about love again
And no longer dream about snakes

Prison Friends
by
Kimeko R. Campbell

Prison friends are like raindrops
They shift when the wind blows
One day you're making plans to kick it on the outs
But like water down the drain your friendship goes

I'd give it a week or two
For the fake smile that people flash at you
To do you wrong in some way or another

People In prison know nothing about loyalty
Don't know how to be a real friend
And only want to use each other

In this place if you spend $180
You'll have all of friends in the world
But just beware cause when there's no more there
You'll once again be a lonely girl

People use you for tobacco soap food
Anything they can get their hands on
They'll sit up under you just long enough
To get what they want and then they're gone

If you are new to this school, you better learn all the rules
Before you get hurt really bad
People don't care about you or what you've been through
They just want everything that you have

So, if you're lonely
And looking for a friend
You best look elsewhere
Don't look in the pen

Because in this place
One day you will have a friend
But a few days later
That friendship is gone with the wind

Chapter 16

Brighter Days

Once I got my transfer, I was already packed up and ready to go. This time there was no call over the loudspeaker for my departure. I had a big cart with all the things I had accumulated over the months. There was no escort. I met the guard at the gate, and he let me go through. So long B-Yard, and fuck all y'all.

C-Yard seemed like a block away. I had to pass the main yard to get to it. When I arrived at the new unit, I was sweating badly. It was very hot in the summertime at Chowchilla. It was always 100 degrees or more during the day. Not to mention that the wheels on the cart that I was pushing kept getting stuck.

C-Yard was different, it was built the same as B-Yard, but the atmosphere was different. It seemed brighter, and I didn't feel the same negative energy as felt on the other yards that I had been on. This yard was much more relaxed.

My new unit was at the very end of the yard, right next to the chow hall. Unit 512, room 11 was my new temporary home. I had to walk across the entire yard to get there. People were greeting me as I was pushing the cart, so I guess my reputation had preceded me. I didn't think that I would know anybody on that yard. The people that I knew and wanted to see were on D-Yard. As soon as I entered the building, a girl named Sneaky, Reno's girlfriend, came running up to me and she hugged me. I was thinking, "Oh great. Now Reno is really going to be jealous because now I'm in the same unit with her ugly girlfriend." I just knew that eventually I was going to have to beat Reno up.

I went to my new room and put my things away. Then I went outside and kicked it with Sneaky. She was all over me, holding on to my arm as we were walking and that made me uncomfortable. I didn't want anyone thinking that we were romantic. As we talked and I got to know her, I found out that she was from Long Beach, CA and she used to date my brother. She had a two-year sentence for forgery. She had already been there for a year. We stayed out for a while, and then I went to my room to settle in and get to know my new roommates.

My new room was okay. There were only four people in there including me. One of my new roommates was leaving, and the other two were a couple named Tina and Cory. Tina was a lifer. She had been down for twenty-two years. She was in for killing two men. She killed the first one when she was eighteen but never got caught. The second man she strangled to death. They labeled her a man-hater and gave her life. Not to take away from her crime, but men do much worse things to women, and I have never heard one of them being labeled as a woman-hater, not even Ted Bundy.

Cory was a young girl. She was down for drugs and was a short termer. At first the room was cool because I wasn't there a lot. I was usually out on the main yard kicking it with the women that I knew from other yards. When I was in the room, I would mostly write. Cory used to clean the room all of the time. It became annoying after a while. She had this thing about wet sinks and would follow me. After I left the sink, she would dry it out. She said that she used to be a maid, but I think she was tweaking. After a while I didn't mind her cleaning. I liked the fact that she liked cleaning, and I only had to clean once a week.

Every day, Sneaky would come to my room, stand at the door, and wait for me to come out. Even early in the morning she would be there so we could go to breakfast together. She always wanted me to go to the main yard with her and I knew why. She had broken up with Reno and wanted to make her jealous, but I wasn't falling for it. I didn't really like going to the main yard too much. I would mostly go to the main yard to walk around the track with Melissa. There were always lots of fights on the main yard, and it would regularly get shut down early for some kind of madness.

One day, I was out on the main yard with Melissa, and she asked me if I had gotten into another fight. She said that she saw a big white girl with a black eye, and she knew that I gave it to her. She was talking about Holly, the devil chick from A-Yard. After five months, Holly still had a black eye and a red dot on the other eye.

Melissa asked me to teach her how to beat people up and give them black eyes. She didn't need to know how, because I would have beaten up anybody that she wanted me to, and I would have made sure to give that person a black eye or two. I never saw Melissa again after that. I think that she went home. I didn't even get the chance to say goodbye to her and we never exchanged information. I pray that she is doing well.

July 16, 2003 was to be my first day working on the PIA (Prison Inmate Assignment) Almond Farm and just like my life, I didn't know what to expect. I was still upset about not going to Fire Camp to be honest but it was a farm so it couldn't be too bad. If nothing else, it paid .22 cents an hour, which was more than any other job paid. I figured if nothing else, I might see a wolf or a snake or a tarantula or even a squirrel. But I didn't.

An officer came to my room at 6:30am and flashed his flashlight at my eyes until I woke up. I didn't like that. He gave me five minutes to come out and then escorted me to the security gate. There were a few women already there waiting. We went through the gate and boarded a van. We drove for about half an hour to an orchard. All I saw was acres and acres of almond trees. I knew that couldn't be good. On one side there was an orange orchard and there were people picking fruit. On the other side there was an almond orchard and that was where I would be working. When I looked at all those almond trees, all I could think about was slavery.

We exited the van and sat on a stone wall for a while until we were divided into groups and then we followed our leader. My group was led to a big building in the center of a large field. I saw a tractor and I thought that it would be cool to learn to drive it. I also saw a loader and I really wanted to learn to drive that. If I had those skills, I could get a good paying job quickly. I asked the leader of our group if we would get a chance to drive the trucks and she said, "Negative." I didn't like that. I never accept no for an answer.

We entered a building that had the word PACKING in large letters on it. Inside, the air smelled of almonds. There was a huge vat full of almonds that had been roasted. There were also several large machines for packing and labeling. It was very loud there because the machines were constantly running. We had to use earplugs most of the time. The only thing good about that building was the air conditioner. Soon I learned my job as an almond packer and got into the flow. I never saw so many almonds before, but I never liked eating almonds, so this was no prize for me. To this day, I despise almonds. Working was hard, and the days were endless. I was completely exhausted by the time I returned to my room.

There was this one inmate who worked there named Cady. She was the only one who was allowed to operate all the machines, including the construction equipment. Cady was being shown too much favoritism, I believed that she and my boss were having an affair. My boss Ms. Etherige would give Cady lighters and let her smoke in her office. Cady would even drive Ms. Etherige's truck from time to time. Cady was a short black woman with a Jerri curl and Ms. Etherige was a tall white woman that looked like Meryl Streep. They made the oddest couple, but I guess it worked for them.

After working as a packer for a few days, I was done with that position. I couldn't quit or I would get into trouble. I had to get them to fire me or give me a medical clearance. One day, while we were in the packing room working, I stood at the almond vat and made sure that everybody was looking at me, and I fainted on purpose.

I was good at it. I laid there on the floor and the girls surrounded me. They were on to me, saying things like, "That looked fake. She's faking." No matter what they said I did not open my eyes until my boss came and used smelling salts to wake me up. That was some good acting. I tried to tell them that I was allergic to almonds, but they didn't fall for that. Instead, they assigned me to work outside in the orchards. I didn't like that either. I felt like a slave out there, especially working in that 120-degree heat. Just awful.

July 30, 2003 was my last day working on the PIA Almond Farm. I was fired for going out of bounds. There are always two versions to every story and here is my version: the morning of July 30, I asked my boss where I was going to be working for the day. She told me to look at the work assignment list. I was working with an inmate named Ferguson, she had been working there for a while. She was a young black girl and only had a few months left to serve. I thought she was cool and was looking forward to working with her. I grabbed some tools and we headed off into the rows of almond trees.

We were supposed to be checking irrigation lines, but she didn't know what she was doing, and neither did I. We walked around, pretending as though we were checking lines, when in reality, we headed to the fence that separated the orchards. Sometimes lighters would get thrown over the fence. The fence was only four feet tall and made of barbed wire. We were looking for lighters when she decided to go one way and I decided to go the other way. Before I knew it, I had walked to a narrow road, and there was an even smaller barbed wire fence. It was so small that I could step over it and walk ten feet to reach the open road.

There was absolutely no reason for me to try to escape though, that just didn't make any kind of sense. I turned around and walked back to the rows. It was extremely hot out there and they had these water stations posted in different parts of the rows, but most of the containers were empty. I was already tired of that job, so I decided to faint in the center of the road. I was going to lay there until someone walked up and spotted me and called for help. I laid out there in the hot sun for fifteen minutes, and no one came. I got up and moved to another spot near a tree and fainted again, still no one came. I decided to try it again the next day. I was on my way back to the irrigation rows when my boss and another lady drove up on an ATV. They pulled up to me and told me to get on. I got on and they drove me back to the office.

Once we got back to the office, Ms. Etherige told me to take off my boots and she searched them. Then she told me I was fired for sleeping, and for going out of bounds. She said that I was sleeping when they pulled up on me and that I tried to escape. That was a total lie. I was going to tell on her for giving the inmates lighters, but it didn't get that far. The citation was dismissed but not without me fighting it all the way. In the end I got what I wanted and that was to get fired! With no additional time.

After I was fired and searched, I was driven back to the prison and escorted to my unit. I was so happy to have gotten fired. I didn't care that it paid .22 cents an hour. I was just happy to not have to ever go back to that farm again. Had I been able to learn to drive those trucks, I would have loved working on the farm. Ms. Etherige issued me a 115 citation. The one thing about the assignments that I never really understood, was why they would give the lifers or the long termer's the best jobs even though they would never be released, and would never be able to use those job skills. I could have used those skills.

I was sent to work in an auto body shop and of course the head person was a lifer. All she allowed me to do was to clean up the shop and take out the trash. She would never teach me how to do anything even though I wanted to learn. She would give her friends the good jobs, and wouldn't even let me hold a can of paint. I told my new counselor Mrs. Rhodes that I couldn't stand the fumes, so I didn't stay there long. There was a video production program that I would have been great at, but the instructor didn't let me into the class. I guess I was too eager, because I pestered him nearly every other day. The instructor straight out told me that he was not letting me into that class and that was that.

Two weeks after I was fired from the Almond Farm, I received notification that my nephew's court arraignment was coming up and that I would need to go to court for it. I would have to leave prison and go to the L.A. County Jail for his court appearance. I didn't think that I had a choice. I wanted to go so that I could make sure that he went to jail for burglarizing my apartment. And mostly because I knew that I could get visits from my mother and friends while I was there. I also wanted to get away from the prison for a couple of weeks.

I already knew that once I left, I would be gone for two weeks. I was starting to get bored, and I was really getting tired of Sneaky and her antics. I was beginning to feel lonely. I would pull out the letters that my friends and my family had written to me. Reading those letters really made me feel better. I appreciated each and every letter that

I received. Some of the women that I had met there even wrote me letters once they got out.

My friend Dee would write to me and tell me that she was waiting for me to get out so that we could go on more Meekster Adventures (finding animals and filming the encounters). My friend Steph would always encourage me to write and to stay positive, and that we would one day make a movie together. My friend Ron would tell me to hang in there, because the fish were only getting bigger, and even the fish were waiting for me to get out to catch them. My dearest friend/sister, Helen was my angel. I can't put into words how much she did for me. I love her so very dearly. My cousin sent me letters, and My friend Tyria, whom I appreciate greatly, wrote to me and sent me money. Lois and Cherry were women that I had met while I was incarcerated, and they wrote to me too. The letters that I loved reading the most were the letters from my mother. They were always so beautiful, and very encouraging.

Letters mean the world to people who are in prison, so if you know anyone serving time, you should write them. Most of the women's biggest complaints were that nobody wrote to them. I would feel guilty at times because I received lots of letters. I was truly blessed. Thank you to all of you who took the time to think about me, and write to me in one of my deepest times of need. I will never forget the love that you have shown me, and I hope and pray that I will be able to one day repay you all. I love you all.

I received my transfer for the following day. I had already been told about taking tobacco with me so that I would have something to sell once I got to the County Jail. I wouldn't be there long enough to receive any money and I was going to need some things from the canteen store. When the day came, I locked up my things, and I was ready to go. I was escorted by an officer through the service gate that led to the big black and white Sheriff bus. They handcuffed me to another woman, this time with no shackles on our ankles. There were only four women on the bus, and in a short time, we were on our way to County Jail Hell.

Wasted Words
by
Kimeko R. Campbell

You said that you loved me
But I know that you don't
You said that you'd wait for me
But I know that you won't.

You said that you'd write me
When you got paroled
I said that I'd miss you
When you went home.

But we both know
That really wasn't true
You didn't write me
And I ain't missing you.

Whatever we had
Has been and gone
I found someone new
So that I wouldn't be alone.

I liked you though
I'm keeping it real with you
Deep down inside
I know you liked me too.

I had your back
If anybody flashed
I'd have lost my day
From kickin' their ass

I can't say that it was worth
All the feelings that I shared
The way that I expressed myself to you
So that you knew that someone cared

I guess I got from you
All that I'm going to get
Because it's been months since you left
And I still haven't heard from you yet

The plans that we made
To kick it on the outs
Were just wasted words
Coming out of your mouth

Chapter 17

County Jail Hell

The first thing that I noticed when I got on the bus was how cold it was. I didn't take a jacket or anything because it was August. The bus seemed to get colder as we drove along, and I huddled with my wrist buddy for warmth. She was really cool and very young. Laura was a white girl serving time for forgery and she was facing another charge for fraud and identity theft.

On the way to the County Jail, Laura and I talked a lot about what was going to happen once we got there. She had been in and out of prison pretty much her whole life. She told me that, when we got to the County Jail, I should request to work in the medical department because once we finished court, the jail deputies would put us in a Pod for medical porters. I liked that idea because I had a medical background and working in a medical jail ward would be a good experience for me to add to my resume once I got out.

Laura also reminded me that I was state property. This meant that I belonged to the State of California and was not a ward of the County. Prisoners that belonged to the State were treated differently than people who were prisoners of the County. The County couldn't lay a hand on us. If they did, they would have to answer for it in a big way and they knew it. The reason for the separation of State and County was that the State was getting paid big dollars for each inmate and the

County didn't get paid as much for the prisoners that were being held there. This was information that I really needed to know.

Laura also told me that the prisoners in County would be expecting the women from prison to be bringing something in, such as tobacco and lighters. The women who were in the County Jail loved to see women from prison come into their Pod. I had to be super careful though. I never knew who I could trust, and I didn't trust anyone. I barely trusted Laura.

Once we exited the freeway, I could instantly smell the stench of the Downtown Los Angeles Skid Row area in the air through the air conditioning vents. What an unpleasant smell. I didn't miss that at all. I did notice the taco trucks and oh how I wanted a carne asada taco. Actually, I wanted ten tacos and a gallon of orange juice. I knew that it would be a very long time until I had a taco and fresh, not from concentrate orange juice.

Before I knew it, we pulled into the County Jail parking garage. It brought back the painful memories of when I was there last. When I stepped off of the bus the stench in the air was confirmed. It was humid and musty and smelled like dead rats mixed with grease. Maybe that smell was coming from the nearest Chinese food restaurant.

When I saw the door to enter the jail, I hesitated to go through it. As soon as the officer opened the door, it was like someone turned on the radio and all I could hear was chaos. People were wrestling with the deputies. Men were screaming and nobody was even doing anything to them. The junkies were walking around scratching themselves and it smelled like ass. This was hell if I ever saw it. I could not wait to get out of there. It was so dirty and full of germs, just disgusting.

This time I didn't have to wait as long as I did the last time I was there. I didn't have to get booked, I only had to be issued another wristband and this one was green. The green wristband identified me as State Property. They couldn't really discipline me the whole time I was in there, and that couldn't have been easy because I became a problem prisoner after a while. They didn't know how to deal with me. I didn't even know how to deal with myself. I had major issues while I was in the county jail, and it was their fault entirely.

We did have to get strip-searched again, but I was a professional at getting stripped and searched by then. I just wanted to get everything over with so that I could settle into whatever Pod that they placed me in. As the deputy pulled me from the holding cell, I got separated from Laura. I never even saw her again. I heard that Laura went back to prison on time, but I did not.

By the time I got to the Pod, I was worn out. I hated everything about that place. The only good thing was seeing and talking to my mother for fifteen minutes when she came to visit me. I was miserable as soon as I walked off that bus. It was like beginning my sentence all over again. I went to one Pod and the girls kept asking me questions and I didn't feel like talking. As soon as the deputy opened the door, I walked out of the Pod. The deputy said, "Get back in there," but I said no. I put my hands behind my back and spread my legs before they could say anything. I already knew the deal. I knew what I was doing. I wanted to go to the Hole, but they didn't want to send me there.

After riding on the bus for six hours and waiting in reception for another eighteen hours, I was super tired and just wanted to sleep. I wouldn't be able to sleep in a loud Pod. I might have ended up getting into another fight. Every time they would take me to a Pod, I would walk in, hear the noise, turn around, and walk out before they could even close the door. I didn't say a word. I would just assume the position. I had to do what I felt like I had to do.

Finally, I gave in on the third Pod because I was thirsty, I had to use the bathroom, and I was exhausted. I climbed onto the first bunk that I could reach. I dared anybody to say anything to me and I fell asleep instantly. The next day, I went upstairs to take a shower and there was a line. I saw towels hanging over the rail, but I didn't care to know what that was about. I stood there for about two minutes when I heard a voice behind me say, "You're in my spot." I turned around and it was a Mexican lady, a boy. I looked at her and, believe it or not, I moved to the next spot. And then I felt a tap on my shoulder, and some other Mexican lady, another boy, said that I was standing in her spot. I said with my Deebo voice, "It's my spot now." She didn't say another word to me. Nobody did.

After a week, I was taken out for court and that was the part that I dreaded the most. I had to go through the same routine all over again, just to sit in court for twenty minutes. The bus ride, the holding tank, the sealed piece of bologna with a hamburger bun for lunch… It was my worst nightmare.

I didn't know how I was going to make it for another week, but I had to manage. For the most part, I kept to myself. And after a week or so, they assigned me a room without a roommate, so I slept most of the time. When I first walked into that tiny cell, the first thing that I noticed was a long, narrow window, so narrow that my arm couldn't fit through it. That long narrow window was the only hope that people had in that place. I couldn't wait until Thursday came so I could go back to prison. Prison was a resort compared to County Jail. I never want to see that place ever again in my life. I don't even want to drive past the building.

On Wednesday night, I was anxious because I was going to take the the "Chain" on Thursday and go back to prison. I listened for my name all night and all morning and they never called it. "What the fuck was going on?" was all I could ask myself. I was at the Pod door pushing the button to the intercom like crazy. They acted like they didn't hear it.

I turned into the Incredible Hulk. I wanted to tell them, "Don't make me angry. You won't like me when I'm angry." I pushed and pushed and kept pushing and banging on the window.

Someone finally answered. "What?"

I said, "I was supposed to have left to go back to Chowchilla this morning."

She paused for a few seconds and said, "They forgot to put you on there."

I wanted to pick somebody up and throw them through the window. I was actually growling. On top of that they had moved some white Ho with AIDS into my room. The Ho in my room was nasty and smelly and I wasn't going to stay in that room with her.

As soon as the door opened, I went out. They opened the doors for people to go into their rooms for the night, but instead I went out of my room and sat at a table. I was the only one out there, just sitting at the table with my hands in the praying position. I wasn't praying but my eyes were closed. I was being 100% defiant. They were going to have to pick me up to move me because I wasn't budging. I didn't have a plan. I just wanted to go to the Hole. I was so incredibly angry with everyone, especially the deputies. And they knew it.

They must have thought that I was going to use karate on them because they put on their riot gear. I saw them running up to the Pod from the corner of my eye. I thought to myself, "It's about to be on." I have no idea where I got so much courage from. I was ready for anything. They knew exactly why I was mad and this time I didn't write a letter.

They opened the door and rushed in and just stood there waiting for me to do something. After about five minutes, I stood up, looked at them, turned around and assumed the position. I put my hands behind my back and let them handcuff me with no problem. I thought for sure that they were taking me to the Hole, but they took me to another Pod instead. They opened the door and pushed me inside and closed the door real fast, before I could even catch my balance and run back out.

I stood at that door for hours pushing that button. Every time they would answer the intercom, I would scream, "I want my shit! I want my shit!" I kept saying that over and over until they said, "What is wrong with you?"

Again I said, "I want my shit". The shit that I was referring to was the newspaper clippings that I had collected during the time I was there. It wasn't much, but they were all that I had, and I wanted them. A few minutes later, the deputy came to the door. She didn't open it, but she slid my newspaper clippings under the door.

I don't think I said one word to anyone in that Pod. I was the angriest person that they had ever seen. One morning, I was laying on the lowest bunk of a three-person bunk bed. The lower bunk almost touched the floor. I didn't even have a sheet – just a blanket, and I don't know how I got that blanket. I think somebody put it over me when I was asleep.

That morning everyone in the Pod needed to be up. I didn't get up. I just laid there on my back with my eyes closed tight. Two deputies walked into the Pod and asked one of the women what my deal was. I heard the girl tell them that I came in with an attitude.

One of the deputies was a woman and the other was a man. They asked me to get up, but I didn't budge, I didn't even open my eyes. They kept asking me with no results. Two more deputies came over to assist in getting me up. I didn't know why they wanted me up so badly, but I just wanted them to leave me alone. They removed my blanket and they saw that I had my hands gripped on each side of the 2-inch mat that I was laying on.

I would not open my eyes and I wouldn't let go of the mat. All four of the officers tried to flip the mat over and roll me off it, but I wouldn't let go. They tried to pry my fists open, but they couldn't do it. Finally, the female deputy kneeled down beside me, and whispered in my ear, "Miss, please just get up and go to breakfast." I opened one eye and looked at her, and she smiled at me. It wasn't her fault so I took a deep breath and I just got up. Anyone else would have gotten beaten up and pepper sprayed.

They sent me back to prison as soon as they could but that wouldn't happen until the following Thursday. I was the only one on the bus. I couldn't wait to leave and I'm sure that everybody in the whole jail couldn't wait for me to leave either. I'm pretty sure that at least one of the jail employees had to answer for the huge mistake that they made. I was just glad to be out of there. I gave County Jail hell.

Chapter 18

Final Destination

The bus ride back was like a limousine ride. I just sat back and enjoyed it. All that I wanted to do was to get back to my room and take a hot shower to wash off those disgusting jail germs. When the bus exited Avenue 22, I got excited! I felt how those other women felt when they were returning to prison and got excited. As we drove down the familiar narrow road and approached the prison grounds, I took in a deep breath. I was happy to see the warning signs and the high voltage fences. As the bus approached the huge entrance gate and I saw the officer in the tower with his rifle, I felt like I was Home Sweet Home. The re-entry process didn't bother me at all. I just couldn't wait to get back to my room and forget about that whole entire trip.

As soon as I got back to the unit, Sneaky came running up to me trying to tell me all about some drama that happened while I was gone. I didn't even listen to her. I was done with Sneaky. All I wanted to do was stay out of trouble and keep a low profile. I didn't know too many people, so I wasn't as popular on C-Yard as I was on the previous yards. Not being so popular gave me the chance to write songs and poems and to focus on my future once I left prison. I only had six months left to serve, and I wasn't going to do anything to interfere with my release.

I was eventually assigned a new counselor and she was really nice. Her name was Mrs. Rhodes. She was married to a yard sergeant who also worked on C-Yard, and he was cool too. He always called me Zap. Not one time did he ever call me Campbell. Mrs. Rhodes pretty much put me in any job that I asked her to. She gave me an office job, but I worked there for two days and didn't like it. The hours were from 9-5, Monday through Friday, and I did not like that. I was never an office type of person. Next.

My next job was working in the kitchen, the chow hall. I actually liked that job. The shifts were split from 4am to 8am and back at 4pm until 8pm. The officer would again come to my window, and flash his flashlight in my eyes to wake me up though. I will never forget that, nor will I ever forget how cold it was outside at 4am during November. I would be frozen by the time I got to work.

Working in the kitchen was cool. It paid eleven cents an hour, but it was fun for the most part. There were eight women who worked with me and there was always something going on. I worked on the tray line mostly. I would add certain foods to the trays as they moved along the line. Every evening I would get the party going by singing *Girls Just Wanna Have Fun* as we were serving the food. The other girls would join in and before long we would have a singing contest going on with the girls on D-Yard. They could hear us and would try to out-sing us. But I knew all the words to too many songs and they didn't.

One of the women that worked in the kitchen with me, really liked me. Her name was Patty. She was serving a seven-year sentence for attempted murder. She caught her fiancé cheating on her, but he didn't know that she knew about it. She tried to put a spell on him but that didn't work. She hired someone to have her fiancé beaten up, but the guy snitched on her. The police found out that she was the mastermind behind the attack and locked her up. She was found guilty and sentenced to seven years. She had been in prison for three years already.

Patty also had a girlfriend named Happy. Patty was a nice-looking lady. She was tall and curvy with long, dark hair. I think that she was Dominican. Her girlfriend Happy, was big and solid. I wouldn't call her fat, but she was solid and thick, and she was Mexican. Happy worked in the kitchen on D-Yard, but the kitchens were connected. Sometimes when the door was open, Happy would come to our side to see Patty. I was cool with both of them.

The other women that worked in the kitchen with me were Sharon, the littlest, toughest person I ever met. She was a tiny black woman with glasses. She wore her hair in a little bun, and she had my back for whatever. There was a woman named LA that worked there as well. All I can say about her was that she was cool. She was the Jill Scott type, and her job was to carry the big food pans back and forth from the oven to refill the food containers, all night. Those big pans had to weigh 25 lbs each. Our boss was an officer named Bliss. He was a tall, slim, white man with a thin mustache and he always wore a green baseball cap. The cap was a part of his uniform.

Sweetie was another woman that worked in the kitchen. She had a big butt, and she could actually make it clap as if she was clapping her hands. This was before twerking became popular. I had never seen anybody that could make their butt clap before or after. And then there was Nita, an older black woman. Her youngest child was twenty-three, but for some reason she could still produce breast milk. She would squirt it at people, and we would all run! There were others but those were the women that I worked with the most.

I remained in unit 512 for about two more weeks until the office could find me a permanent room. I was getting moved around so much that I had gotten used to it. All I knew was that time was moving forward, and that was the most important thing to me. It wasn't like I had that many things to pack. Everything that I owned fit into a regular sized drawer and a high school sized locker. I got moved out of that unit and was on to the next adventure.

The room that I was in was a transient room. I stayed in that room until I would be permanently housed in unit 510- 30-2up. This unit would be my final destination. The room was cool from the moment that I stepped inside. There were only three people there, two boys and one girl. They were all black and I didn't feel any tension at all. They welcomed me right away. There was Stephanie, a skinny, super dark skinned, cracky looking woman. She had "Crack Head" written all over her body. She didn't even need to tell me her story. I could have told her own story.

Then there was Casanova, a lifer who lived her life as a man. She had a Flava Flav kind of look. She had been down for twenty-three years for murdering her pimp. She had a son who was twenty-three who used to come and visit her. She was pregnant with her son when she killed her pimp. Her story was that her pimp used to beat her up a lot and she was afraid of him. She said that he would smoke crack and do crazy things. One night, her pimp beat her up and told her to shoot a guy that he had kidnapped and taken behind a building. He told her that if she didn't shoot the guy that he would kill her and the baby. She shot her pimp instead of shooting the guy, and the guy went to the police and told what happened. She was serving a life sentence for that.

And then there was T-Bird, a boy. T-bird reminded me of JJ ("Dynomite") Jimmy Walker from the show Good Times. T-Bird was a thief and not a very good one. She was serving a life sentence for stealing two pairs of boxer shorts from JC Penney. I could see how she got caught because she was a terrible thief. She couldn't even steal butter from the chow hall for me without looking suspicious. The fact that she got life was just vicious. Shame on the seriously flawed justice system. Her first two strikes were for attempted robbery.

The first strike that she got was for stealing an old man's wallet. The old man caught her, beat her with his cane, and held her down until the police came. The second strike was for snatching a woman's purse. She snatched a woman's purse, and tripped on the curb and was unconscious until the police arrived. I'm not saying that she doesn't need to be punished, but not for the rest of her life. Most men who murder and rape children don't get life in prison. Not even if they rape and kill an infant. The law is way more lenient on male crimes, and men commit the worst crimes imaginable.

Other people would come and go but me, Casanova, and T-Bird remained in the same room the whole time I was there. Over time we could get another roommate who would stay. Her name was Cookie, I called her Lil Baby. She was only seventeen years old. She was serving thirty-seven years for murder. When Lil Baby first arrived, she didn't say much. She was really skinny and frail, and she was so sad about her time. I couldn't imagine what kind of crime that she could have committed that was so terribly bad. She was so little and meek and frail that I couldn't picture her doing anything bad at all.

I made her feel welcome and I took a liking to her. One night when we were alone, I let Lil Baby sit on my bed. We started talking and I asked her to tell me her story. She told me that she had been accused of killing an old lady. Let me quote her. "My crime involved an ice shovel, a bolt wrench, a pipe wrench, and an ax."

On July 21, 2000, Lil Baby was at home relaxing. Her mother had gone shopping and told her not to go anywhere. She was only fifteen years old, so her older brother was there babysitting her. The telephone rang and it was Nita, Lil Baby's younger friend. Nita was the one person that Lil Baby's mother had told her not to associate with. Nita told Lil Baby that she wanted her to go somewhere with her. She told Nita that she couldn't leave until her mother came home. Lil

Baby hung up the phone. Nita kept calling, telling her that it was an emergency. Finally, Nita convinced her to disobey her mother and go over to her house.

Nita lived about a mile away from Lil Baby, so they met each other halfway. Once they met up, they went to the store and bought some candy bars and soda. On the way back to Nita's house, they passed the house of an old cat lady. The old lady was in her yard chasing after her cats. Nita asked Lil Baby, "Do you want to see me kill somebody?"

Lil Baby replied, "What? No."

"Come on," Nita tells Lil Baby, "let's go get one of them kittens. I want a kitten."

They crossed the street and entered the old lady's gate and walked up to her porch. The old lady was standing in her doorway. Nita approached the old lady and asked her for a kitten. The lady said yes if you can catch one.

Lil Baby was standing behind Nita and a kitten ran past the old lady into the house. Nita went past the old lady and followed the kitten into the house. The old lady told Nita to get out of her house, but she didn't listen. Instead, she went further inside of the house. The old lady followed Nita into the house and Lil Baby followed them both. Lil Baby said that the first thing that she noticed as she looked around the house, was that there were lots of old newspapers everywhere, and there was a big red toolbox that was open. Lil Baby said that the toolbox had big tools in it and Nita went over to the toolbox, and started playing with the tools.

Lil Baby said that Nita grabbed a pipe wrench and by this time the old lady had walked down the hallway to her room. Lil Baby followed Nita down the hallway and looked in the bedroom. The old lady was sitting on her bed, and Nita raised the pipe wrench above her head and hit the lady in the face so hard that blood spattered onto the ceiling.

She said that she could see the blood dripping from the wrench as Nita kept hitting her. She said that the old lady was bent over backward on her bed, and Nita went to the toolbox and got another tool and went back into the bedroom and continued to beat the woman.

Nita hit the old lady so hard with a bolt wrench that she knocked the lady's dentures down her throat. Lil Baby said that Nita kept going to the toolbox to get different tools to beat the lady with. Lil Baby said that she never went into the bedroom but saw it all from the end of the hallway. Lil Baby said that she was terrified of Nita and didn't know what to do. They left and went to Nita's house.

By that time, it was getting dark outside. A car load of their friends pulled up next to them as they were walking. The friends in the car asked them where they were going and noticed blood all over the two of them. The friends in the car asked it if they had been playing with ketchup and they both said yes. Nita said that they had a food fight, and the car drove off. Once they got to Nita's house, no one saw them go into the bathroom to clean themselves up. Lil Baby couldn't explain to me how she got blood on her.

After they had cleaned themselves, they went to the living room and started watching the movie *Friday the 13th*. Nita told Lil Baby that she didn't think that the old lady was dead and that they needed to go back and make sure. Lil Baby said she had no choice but to go because she was scared of Nita. They went back to the old lady's house and went inside. Nita went straight to the toolbox, grabbed an ax, and went into the bedroom. Lil Baby stood in the hallway and watched. Nita went up to the old lady who was still laying on the bed bent over backward. Nita raised the ax above her head and smashed it so hard into the old lady's abdomen that she rose up and started gurgling. Nita raised the ax again and smashed the poor old lady in the head, slicing her head open, and killing her!

That was by far the most horrific story that I had ever heard in prison. And it didn't end there. After Nita had killed the lady, they went back to Nita's house. Later that night, Nita left to go to the movies to see Scream and Lil Baby stayed at her house. It was too dark for Lil Baby to walk home, and Nita had told her to stay at her house for the night. Lil Baby was scared and did not know what to do.

Nita's older sister came home, and Lil Baby told the sister everything. The sister was terrified as she listened to the details and called her mother, who immediately rushed home from work. Lil Baby told Nita's mother what happened, and the mother called the police. The police arrested Lil Baby and later arrested Nita at the movie theater.

The police interrogated Lil Baby without her parents being present, and without a lawyer present. They got a confession from Lil Baby but not from Nita. Nita's mom had hired a lawyer for her. Since Nita was thirteen at the time of the crime and Lil Baby was fifteen, the prosecutor went after the secured conviction for Lil Baby, and won. Lil Baby received 37 years.

One day, I was in the day-room with Lil Baby, and we were watching *The Simpsons* cartoon. This just so happened to be an episode where Lisa Simpson was doing a report on a crazy lady who owned a lot of cats. In the cartoon, Lisa set up her camera in front of the crazy cat lady's house. All of a sudden, the cat lady runs outside like a wild woman with cats all over her head and shoulders and chases Lisa away by throwing cats at her. I couldn't help but look at Lil Baby and burst out laughing. If you ever see that episode, you will burst out laughing too, even without knowing the story. She didn't think it was funny at all. If I were in her position, I wouldn't have thought that it was funny either.

The next day I apologized to her, and it all was good. I did feel bad because she never joked about her crime. She had hopes that her appeal would go through, and she would get out. She really was a sweet girl who had a terribly bad set of circumstances come at her. I tried my best to encourage her. I didn't let anyone mess with her either. Cookie was my Lil Baby.

There I was pouting and complaining about doing eighteen months and that seemed like such a long time. Now my time was almost up. I thought about all of the people that would still be in prison serving their time after I was long gone. Life in prison means prison is your life, forever. Living in a room with seven strangers, forever. All of your possessions have to fit in a drawer and a locker forever. Sleeping on an iron bed with a 5-inch mattress forever. Hearing the alarms and the threats over the loudspeaker forever. Never seeing what's beyond these gates forever.

I thought that most lifers would be like the bullies in the movies, angry and miserable. But actually, the lifers that I met had a better attitude than the short termers did. I guess that once they accepted their fate, there was nothing else for them to do but live with it or commit suicide. Before I got locked up, I never put too much thought into women serving life sentences. Now that I have lived with them, heard their stories, and shared food with them, I realize that they are just women who made really bad choices, and that could happen to any one of us at any given time. Make sure that you always stop and think before you act. Think about being in prison for the rest of your life, and that should stop you. I would have learned my lesson with probation.

I was really getting the feel of my job in the kitchen. I had come a long way since the first night when I got caught stealing a loaf of bread. I tried to walk out of the kitchen with a whole loaf of bread between my legs. The officer who searched me and found it even laughed. I didn't really have to steal anymore because my friend Patty, who worked with me in the kitchen, was having an affair with my boss, Officer Bliss.

They were using me as a cover. I had been getting lighters and anything I wanted from the kitchen.

I suspected that they were having sex, and then she actually confessed to me. She even showed me love letters that he wrote to her. Patty showed me a love letter that she had written. I thought that she wrote that letter to her girlfriend Happy, but she told me that she wrote the letter for Bliss. I knew that this wasn't going to be good for me, because they had been using me as a cover.

I began to despise him because he was married, and he was just using us for his selfish needs. My silence was worth more than a cigarette lighter, and a bag of flour tortillas. He could have at least given me some weed or some liquor. Bliss knew what he was doing, and he knew that Patty had a girlfriend, and that it would fall back on me. I did not like that. I was pissed at her too. She knew what she was doing as well.

I hadn't gotten into any trouble. I liked my job. I didn't have anybody after me or jealous of me because of their girl. The closest I came to a girlfriend was when I used to flirt with an officer named Gonzalez that worked nights with me in the kitchen. When she would release me from work, I would tell her to search between my legs because I had something down there. She would always say, "Whatever it is, you can keep it."

I tried not to let anything get to me. I stayed in my room and wrote when I wasn't working. I didn't even go to the main yard. The only person I hung out with was my friend Tangy, my home girl that I met in County Jail. She thought that I was undercover when she first met me, because she witnessed the fight that I had with Tammy. She truly believed that I worked for the CIA. Tangy wanted me to be the godmother of her children. I could not accept that responsibility.

The holidays approached and people were getting happy because once a year at Christmas, the inmates could order KFC. I always hated

KFC, even out of prison. The chicken in prison tasted better. I only had about 90 days left, and I was good. I didn't want to think about anything else. I couldn't think about anything else. I had nothing else to think about... until I met Cindy.

Chapter 19

Cindy

I was working in the chow hall by myself one night. I was mopping the floor and minding my own business. Patty and Bliss were on the other side of the kitchen having sex. For some reason, I looked out of the window that faced the track, and I saw a few women walking along the track. One of the women looked through the window and waved at me, so I waved back.

I didn't think anything of it and continued mopping. The next night as I was wiping the tables, I noticed that the same woman was looking through the window and waving at me again. This time I recognized her from my unit. She was wearing makeup and she looked really pretty. I waved back with a big smile.

I was almost done with work, and I wanted to time it right so that I would be leaving by the time she came back around the track. I knew that she would come back. Normally I procrastinated leaving work, especially when Officer Gonzales was working but that night was different. When she opened the door, I didn't flirt with her. I started walking with the woman who waved at me. She introduced me to her friend Stranger, and then she told me that her name was Cindy.

I told her that Cindy was a white girl's name and that I expected her name to be Maria or something. She told me that my name sounded like I worked in a Chinese massage parlor, and she expected my name to be Monifah. Cindy had a great sense of humor and I liked that. We talked and talked and before I knew it, we had walked around the track four times. Stranger left, and we didn't even notice. We stayed out on the yard talking until the yard closed. We lived in the same unit, and her room was two doors down from mine. Her story was that she caught her boyfriend cheating on her and she threw a Molotov cocktail bomb at his house. Twice. That was it. I didn't judge people. The Molotov seemed to be her weapon of choice.

Cindy was beautiful even without makeup. She was perfect, and I liked everything about her. She was Mexican, about 5'5, 135 lbs. She had long, thick, pretty, black hair and full lips. She was the only woman that got my attention the whole time I was there, and she was the only woman who deserved it. The problem was that she was talking to somebody else.

I only had two months left by that time, so her talking to someone else was disappointing, but I was ready to go home. I left the situation with Cindy alone. Until one night an officer brought Cindy to my room. I was totally surprised! Turns out that a window had been broken out in Cindy's room, so she was temporarily moved into my room.

Cindy had an upper bed right across from mine. There was nothing to separate us. We stayed up the entire night just talking, mostly. When the guard came to get me for work, I was already up. He didn't have to shine the light in my eyes. I didn't go to sleep that night at all. Cindy brought me joy in a place where I didn't have any at all. And I really liked that. She was the only person that I told the true nature of my crime to. I never told anyone else that I was in there for a squirrel, because that just didn't make any sense at all. Those women were there for cutting off people's heads.

One day, Mr. Rhodes saw me and said, "Come here Zap. There was a fight in your unit. Let me see your knuckles." Zap was the only nickname that I ever got the whole time that I was there. Ceze called me Mac-EzE, but I didn't like that too much. I tried to give myself a nickname but that didn't work either. I went from Punch to Peace but then I just stayed with Meko. I'm glad that I did because nobody would have remembered me by my self-given nickname.

Cindy had been in my room for three days and by the time she left, she wasn't talking to that other girl anymore. She was my girlfriend. Cindy didn't care what people thought about her either. Her favorite words were "I don't give a fuck." We hit it off well and everybody seemed to like us together. We were really cute too. We would walk to dinner together and when we would be in line, she would stand behind me and wrap her arms around my waist and lay her head into my back. I loved it when she did that. I knew that people were secretly jealous of us and hating us. Especially Patty. She used to call herself my wife, so I know that she was super jealous.

Most of the Mexican women loved me because I would bring them whole packs of flour tortillas and beans and salsa. All I wanted in return was whatever they were making. They used to make the best tamales that I ever had, and they used a mop bucket to cook them in. Their burritos were very good too.

Everything was great between me and Cindy for about a month. Tension had been building up in the kitchen between Patty and Happy. Somehow, I was in the center of it. I only had forty-five days and a wake up left on my sentence, and I was not going to get involved in any mess at all.

Happy started thinking that I was messing around with Patty because we were always in the kitchen together, and Patty was always staying at work past her work hours. They lived in the same room, so Happy was suspicious.

Happy never thought that Patty was fucking Bliss. She thought that Patty was having sex with me. I was going to write a letter to the prison board and tell on Bliss and Patty, but Patty begged me not to.

She said that she would take care of things with Happy. I told Cindy all about it, and she wanted to beat Patty up, because at first, she thought Patty and I were having sex too.

I told Cindy to stay out of it because I didn't want to make a big deal about it. I knew that this could cause racial tension. Happy figured that since she was Mexican that she could hang out with Cindy when I was at work. I knew what she was doing. She was using her Mexican card to make me jealous. It didn't work because Cindy told me what was going on.

It was February 3, 2004, and I had less than six weeks and a wake up left on my sentence. Things were looking up. It was a bright beautiful morning, and I went to work. The yard was very busy because, just like in real life, people were off to their jobs and school. There were people lined up for breakfast, and there were a few people already inside the chow hall waiting for us to start serving food. Most of the people that worked in the kitchen were on the other side of the chow hall getting coffee or checking their positions. No one from any other kitchen was supposed to be in there.

Patty and Bliss were standing in the kitchen near the kitchen door, talking in plain sight. Bliss wasn't paying attention to anything else but Patty. I was on the chow hall side of the door about to go into the scullery to turn on the machine, but Happy cut me off before I could go in there. When Happy stood in front of me I told her to stay away from Cindy. She told me to stay away from Patty.

I asked her the wrong question, because I asked her "What if I don't?" She had a coffee mug in her hand, and she cracked me in the forehead, hard. My first thought was that I lost my day. I started socking her in the face. She hit me back in the face a couple of times, but I kept dodging her punches and landing all my punches. She tried to grab my hair, but I grabbed her by her big, football shoulders and spun her into the coffee machines. We were throwing down. By this time Bliss realized we were fighting and started fumbling with his keys to open the door.

I flipped her onto the table, and I got on top of her and started counting the punches to her face. I had blacked out again. I heard nothing, and I only saw her face as I was hitting it. My inner voice said, "Don't let her get up, if she does, she will beat you up." I made sure that she couldn't get up because I straddled her on the table, and I did not stop swinging. I felt a light mist hit my face and I still kept hitting her. I felt another blast of something hit my face. It was pepper spray.

I instantly stopped hitting her and got up and walked over to another table and sat down. I put my hands behind my back, and they came over and handcuffed me. My eyes were burning so bad. The weirdest thing about that fight was that I blacked out again. When I was hitting her, I didn't hear the alarms going off all over the prison. I didn't know that there were twenty cops standing around watching us fight, telling us to stop! They used seven cans of pepper spray on us. And I lost my day.

After they handcuffed me, one of my favorite Sergeants, Lucy, took me to her office. She escorted me across the yard in handcuffs, and it totally reminded me of when I got arrested on A-Yard. Everybody from all across the yard, from every room in every unit was looking at me, and everybody knew what happened. I was super popular after that fight, in a bad way though. Lucy put me and Happy in separate cages. Then she sat there in front of the cages and kept talking to us until we both admitted that we were stupid and that everything was squashed. We agreed, and she let us go. Patty and Cindy were waiting for us to come out. Happy and I apologized to each other. We remained cool, but too much damage was done.

I won the fight, but I felt so damn numb. Cindy hadn't said one nice word to me, because the Mexicans were making her choose or else they would make it hard for her once I was gone. I knew that I had to let her go. I made it easy for her and broke up with her two weeks after the fight. She still had six months left and I knew how the Mexicans would treat her if she stayed with me. If it was meant to be, we would reconnect outside of prison. Before I left, Cindy tried hard to talk to me, but I didn't want to talk. There was really nothing to say. I was just waiting for tomorrow, because tomorrow was only a day away.

Tomorrow Is Only a Day Away
by
Kimeko R. Campbell

Tomorrow in prison
Could mean a week
So I will lay low
And play hide and seek

I won't say too much
I'll keep a low profile
I'm not talking to anyone
I'll just wave and smile

Tomorrow is only a day away
But I'm concerned with surviving today
People are cruel and they don't play
They could be waiting to take my tomorrow away

Anything can happen
To make me stay
I can't get too comfortable
I have to play it safe

Who knows what awaits me
On the other side of that door
It could be something
Chilling to the inner core

Tomorrow just might not come my way
So tonight I will get on my knees and pray
For the Lord to open the gate for me
So I can step out and finally be set free

Chapter 20

Tomorrow Is Only a Day Away

The fight that I had with Happy must have been the best fight that the officers had ever seen, because not one of the twenty officers that were standing around tried to stop it. They watched it for a long time. They were still talking about it a month later. Every time an officer would see me, they would apologize for the pepper spray. I wasn't mad at them at all. I liked most of them and I knew that they liked me a lot. One of the female officers told me that she was trying her hardest not to spray me in the face, and that every officer in the whole prison had to take a new course in handling fights and pepper spray methods.

Officer Schwartz saw me walking, and he caught up with me. He said, "Campbell, I heard you did a Mike Tyson." I have to admit that was the best fight I ever had in my whole entire life, and I had quite a few fights in my life. I had like 11-0 statistics if you count the fights that I had with little boys in elementary school and with my sister. I could have been a professional fighter. I wish that I could have gotten a copy of the video of that fight. I'm sure the prison had video cameras. That was a real fight, and we were basically trading blows. But she wasn't landing her blows because I was dodging them. I didn't have a scratch on me, but she had two black eyes and a lot of knots on her face. Happy was much bigger than me, and she outweighed me by at least 100 plus pounds. I only weighed 145 pounds, but I was fast and strong.

One officer said, "All I know is that I saw the little one kicking the big one's ass." Officer Gonzales couldn't wait to see me. She said, "I heard that you got into a fight and got beat up."

I told her that she heard the wrong story.

She said, "I heard that you had a black eye."

I said, "That was the other girl. She has two black eyes so get your stories straight." Her jaw dropped open and she walked away.

Patty saw me and she ran up to me, and wrapped her arms around my waist to hug me. She said, "Oh my goodness, you are so skinny. I can almost wrap my arms around you twice. How the hell did you give my girlfriend two black eyes?"

I was still mad at Patty, and I wouldn't talk to her. Bliss was being very nice to me because he knew that I was about ready to tell on him. I had already written the letter.

Surprisingly, I didn't get fired. I tried to appeal the citation for fighting based on the fact that Happy was out of bounds. She was not supposed to be in the kitchen that day and Bliss didn't regulate like he was supposed to. The captain said that it basically didn't matter because it was considered mutual combat. He said, "You don't even look like you've been in a fight, but she looks like she just came back from a battle." He pulled out the body charts and she had check marks all over her body. I only had two or three check marks on my body. I could have and should have appealed his decision.

I received thirty days extended stay. The system is lenient with people who start fights, and hard on the people who win the fights. It seemed like I couldn't win from winning. As soon as I walked out of the captain's office, an officer named Rios saw me and said, "Campbell, I heard that you got rained on." He was referring to the rain of pepper spray. I just looked at him and shook my head.

My roommates Casanova, T-bird, and Lil Baby, were very protective of me at that point. They were all mad at Cindy because they felt that the fight was all because of her. They told her to make things right. This was not Cindy's fault and she really tried to make it right with everyone. Even though we had broken up, the Mexicans still weren't satisfied. They wanted her to prove to them that she was done with me. I tried to help Cindy prove it by hanging out with other women, but Cindy would get jealous and sometimes she would sneak into my room, and we would kiss.

One day, I saw Cindy on the yard with a Mexican woman named Lucky. Lucky was in Cindy's face as if she was very interested in her. I didn't say anything to either of them, but as I walked past, I looked at Cindy and smiled and then I gave Lucky the evil eye. The next day at breakfast, I was working in the scullery dumping food trays into the garbage can. Lucky came to the scullery, peeked her head in, and asked for some milk. I told her no. Later she sent one of her friends to ask me for milk and I gave it to her. I saw the girl go to the table where Lucky was sitting, and she handed Lucky the milk. I waited for the two of them to finish eating and slide me their trays.

I had a handful of grits, beans, eggs, and whatever else we had for breakfast packed in my hand. As soon as Lucky walked past the scullery, I flung the handful of food in her face! It landed perfectly. I saw grits and beans sliding down her face. She was very angry. All of us working in the kitchen were laughing our asses off. Lucky didn't do anything except run back and tell Cindy.

Q was my newest roommate, she really had my back. She was really tall and super dark-skinned, and she looked like Bernie Mac. As my day to leave was getting closer, I could feel the tension, especially during my last fifteen days. I was on edge with everyone. I didn't trust a single person. Lil Baby was tripping big time. She had tried to commit suicide three times. She was really jealous of me and Cindy's relationship from the start. Q told me that, one day when I was at work, Lil Baby had gone psycho in the room. Q said that Lil Baby was saying that she was going to do something to hurt me and Cindy. Q told me to be very careful, and by the look on her face, she was very concerned about my safety. Thank God in Heaven that Lil Baby got moved soon after she made that comment. I was starting to believe that she had more to do with that old lady's death than she said.

I felt very delicate as my last few days approached. One night I was working on the tray line, and I had a major attitude because Patty kept trying to talk to me. The officer working that night was Officer Tyra and I liked him. I already had a reputation for fainting, and I was going to faint that night to avoid hurting Patty's feelings. Patty had written me letters apologizing, but she was just doing that so that I wouldn't tell on her and Bliss. If they were exposed, Bliss would get escorted off the grounds and Patty would be sent to another prison. I did write a letter, but I never sent it.

Officer Tyra asked me what was wrong with me because I wasn't myself. I told him that I was mad at Patty. He said, "Campbell, don't be like that, just sing your favorite song." My favorite song to sing was *Lights* by Journey. I was not about to sing. I told him that if he didn't keep Patty away from me, that I was going to faint. His eyes got wide because he knew that I would do it. He said, "Please don't do it on my shift. I only have an hour left." I told him that I liked him and that I would wait, but for him to keep Patty away from me.

When I first got to prison, there was a black girl that I used to walk with who hated Mexicans. She said that Mexicans were more racist than white people. I didn't believe her because I thought that Mexicans and blacks were close to each other, and I like Mexican people a lot. She was right though, because I saw for myself how racist the Mexicans were. The most racist Mexicans were the elders. They had generational prison rules and if you were Mexican and you didn't follow their racist rules, you got totally mistreated, and would receive no protection from them at all.

My time was pretty much served. I had one day and a wake up left, and I was out of there. It was crunch time and it seemed like everything that I did was a potential reason for me to get more time. I tried to wash my clothes and the officer threatened me about something. If I walked outside, I would get threatened. The pressure was on. My only real escape was the scullery in the chow hall.

One day, I was taking a break from work, and I was sitting in the scullery smoking a cigarette. That was the best cigarette that I could remember smoking. I was taking deep drags and taking my time blowing out the smoke. Out of the corner of my eye, I spotted someone wearing green creeping up on me. It was Sergeant Lucy.

She sat right next to me and I kept smoking. She said, "You do know that I'm sitting right next to you right?"

I said, "Yeah, I know, but I'm already in trouble so I might as well finish my cigarette."

She said, "Put it out Campbell." Before she left, she turned around and told me not to light that cigarette back up, and that she had to write me up for it. I didn't get any extra time. She just ordered me to stay in my room for the rest of the night, and I was super good with that.

When I first started serving my sentence, I used to get jealous of women who had gotten their ducat to parole. I was happy for them, but I couldn't wait until my parole day came. The thing about the other women that got paroled was that they would usually come right back to prison, sometimes within weeks. I guess it was hard for them to stay out of trouble, especially when they were addicted to drugs and crime. That's why prison is called a "Revolving Door."

My last day had finally arrived and all I had was a wake up left. I was hoping that I did wake up. I couldn't wait to go home. I didn't really feel nervous until that final day. I had knots in my stomach, and hadn't slept the whole night. I had already said goodbye to everyone, but it was hard to say goodbye to my roommates. They had been my family for the last seven months and I had grown to love them. I hated the fact that they would be in there for the rest of their lives, but I would always tell them that there was always hope.

I didn't know if I was really leaving the next day or not. Anything could have happened to make me stay. I asked Officer Payne a few times if my parole ducat came. Each time that I asked, she would look through the ducats and shake her head no. If the parole ducat didn't come by 9pm, most likely I wouldn't be going home the next day.

Right before it was time for me to go to my room for the night, I went to the officer's kiosk and asked Officer Payne again if my parole ducat had come. This time she smiled. She shook her head yes, and I will never forget the look on her face – she was happy for me. I was so happy that I can't even describe the feeling. I did a full cartwheel right in the center of the day-room.

Officer Payne handed me the ducat and said, "Don't come back." The ducat was a little piece of paper and it read, "Campbell 96217 Paroles." Praise God in Heaven! The Meekster was about to leave the prison. No more unlocks, no more chow hall, no more plastic utensils, no more unit recalls, no more main yard, no more alarms and wondering who was fighting. No more fighting. No more ugly women. No more hooch. No more shower shoes or 115's. It was over. I could learn to live again. The first thing that I wanted was ten carne asada tacos, con queso, a carne asada burrito, and a big bottle of orange juice and a gallon of water.

Tomorrow was my big day. It felt so good to be leaving. I had my last chicken dinner with black-eyed peas and rice, and it was delicious.

Ironically, I had the same dinner the first day that I arrived. I stole my last bag of ice, and it was delicious. I didn't think that I would be able to sleep, but I did, and I slept well. I don't even think that I had a dream. I was at peace for the first time in years.

On 4-20-2004, the day of my parole, I woke up bright and early. People came to my room to say goodbye, and to give me the mail that they wanted me to send off for them. Everyone came to say goodbye, except Cindy. She did give me a letter as I was leaving. She had her roommate Cheeky give it to me. I had given all my possessions away to my roommates. I only kept my paperwork. As I walked across the yard for the last time, all kinds of memories – good, bad, happy, sad – went through my head.

As I approached the exit gate, I had a feeling of uncertainty run through me. I felt tense. When I walked across the threshold, I could taste freedom on my tongue. When I heard that gate slam closed behind me, I knew that my time had been served. It felt so good to know that I was finally free and going home. I took a deep breath, and praised God in Heaven, that I would no longer have to live inside of four walls made of stone.

4 Walls Made of Stone
by
Kimeko R. Campbell

Beyond these prison gates
I live inside of four walls made of stone
They remind me everyday
Of how much I miss my home

For now, my home is inside of this room
And it's filled with heartache, loneliness, and gloom
Some of my roommates are in here for life
And I hear their tears fall as they cry through the night

Some of them are in here
For crimes they did not commit
Some for killing their pimp or rapist
Or some other fucked up shit

Being in this place it ain't nothing nice
Most women comfort themselves by getting a prison wife
Overcoming the fear of being here forever and a day
Hoping that your sentence gets overturned somehow someway

Sleeping on a 5-inch mattress
On top of a metal slab that's cold and hard as a brick
My back and body are truly aching
My mind is starting to feel sick

Waking up every day with nothing to look forward to
Hoping to get a letter from someone who encourages you
No birthday wishes no holiday card
I guess I'll go watch a fight out on the main yard

Saturday and Sunday are just another day
So I pull out my pen
And mark the calendar
To see how much time has passed away

When I first arrived here
Things seemed so strange
Now I look at myself
And I see how much I've changed

This is my new world now
And how quickly I've adapted
I've learned a new way of life
And picked up a few bad habits

The way I walk is different
The way I talk ain't the same
Instead of using proper English
I now use prison slang

I used to say "How are you?"
Now I say wud up fool
If you would look at me, I'd smile
Now I say "What you lookin' at? What you wanna do?"

I can't get into any more trouble
I've already had three fights
Even the warden told me to be careful
Or I could easily end up being in here for life

Now I'm just waiting for the day
When they call my name to go home
I can't wait to wake up and look around
And not be surrounded by four walls made of stone

Being incarcerated for the first time
Has taught me to be the criminal that I never used to be
I wonder how long it will take for me to regroup
Once I am finally set free

Will I have a messed-up attitude?
Or will I return to the same ole me?
I wonder just how or what way
I will deal with modern society

One thing I do know
That I will never do
Is forget where I've been
Or what I have been through

See, I have been truly blessed because I'm going home
But I will always remember the friends that I'm leaving behind
To do the rest of their time
Inside of four walls made of stone

www.ingramcontent.com/pod-product-compliance
Lightning Source LLC
Chambersburg PA
CBHW020520290526
45786CB00002B/694